THE MORAL MAJORITY AND FUNDAMENTALISM

Plausibility and Dissonance

THE MORAL MAJORITY AND FUNDAMENTALISM

Plausibility and Dissonance

Sharon Linzey Georgianna

Studies in Religion and Society
Volume 23
The Edwin Mellen Press
Lewiston/Lampeter/Queenston

Library of Congress Cataloging-in-Publication Data

Georgianna, Sharon Linzey, 1949-
   The moral majority and fundamentalism : plausability and
dissonance / by Sharon Georgianna.
       p.   cm.   --   (Studies in religion and society ; vol. 23)
   Bibliography: p.
   ISBN   0-88946-851-6
   1. Moral Majority, Inc.   2. Fundamentalism.   3. Christianity and
politics--History--20th century.   4. Conservatism--United States-
-History--20th century.   5. United States--Church history--20th
century.   6. United States--Politics and government--1977-1981.
7. United States--Politics and government--1981-1989.   I. Title.
II. Series: Studies in religion and society (New York, N.Y.) ; v.
23.
BT82.2.G46   1989
261.8'0973--dc20   89-36103
                                                              CIP

This is volume 23 in the continuing series
Studies in Religion and Society
Volume 23 ISBN 0-88946-851-6
SRS Series ISBN 0-88946-863-X

A CIP catalog record for this book
is available from the British Library.

        The Edwin Mellen Press   The Edwin Mellen Press
               Box 450   Box 67
            Lewiston, NY   Queenston, Ontario
            USA 14092   CANADA L0S 1L0

                  The Edwin Mellen Press, Ltd.
                    Lampeter, Dyfed, Wales,
                  UNITED KINGDOM SA48 7DY

              Printed in the United States of America

Table of Contents

THE MORAL MAJORITY AND FUNDAMENTALISM

Plausibility and Dissonance

Introduction

"The Moral Majority...The New Right...New Religious Right...New Christian Right....Whatever names it's called, the Extreme Right is raising unprecedented amounts of money, recruiting unprecedented numbers of people and posing an unprecedented threat to individual rights in America today." So says a recent circular from the American Civil Liberties Union. Such was the furor among the more "leftist" thinkers after the 1980 Presidential election. Mainstream social thinkers were appalled and frightened over the power and influence that they perceived this "new right" contingency to have in society. In a matter of a few years these thinkers calmed down, realized that much was show and shrewd use of media resources than actual political power. The New Right was then disdained because they were not nearly as powerful as the illusion they were able to create.

Of all the literature written by authors who are concerned with the New Religious Right's entrance to the politically active world, little attention has been paid to the fact that many participants of the New Religious Right (NRR) are themselves bothered by their own engagement in sociopolitical activism.

Numerous works have been published about the "New Right" which describe the political perspectives and goals of New Right organizations (i.e., Gannon, 1981; Shriver, 1982; McIntyre, 1979; Crawford, 1980; Johnson & Tamney, 1982; Pierard, 1983; Erling, 1981; Yinger & Cutler, 1982; Rater, 1982; Shupe & Stacy, 1982; Webber, 1981; Quebedeaux, 1982; Koenig & Boyce, 1983; Cable, 1984; Harrell, 1981; McGuire, 1982; Hadden & Swan, 1981; Neuhaus, 1984; Liebman & Wuthnow, 1983; Hill & Owen, 1982, and others). None of these studies adequately address the issue that fundamentalists may *themselves* be bothered by their own foray into politics. The neglect of this problem constitutes a fundamental flaw in the treatment of the politics of fundamentalists currently engaged in social action.

Contrary to popular opinion, before the fundamentalist-modernist controversy developed in the first quarter of the twentieth century, social concern and evangelism tended to go hand in hand. It wasn't until the Scopes Trial in the mid 1920's that fundamentalists by and large retreated from the sociopolitical domain and adopted a policy of "separation from the world." When liberal Protestant churches substituted social betterment and the Social Gospel for spiritual redemption, fundamentalist churches became preoccupied with private saintliness, preaching "Christ crucified" in absolute isolation from sociopolitical affairs, and promoted the piety of the local church in total unconcern over social disorders and evils (Henry, 1964:16). For the half century following the Scopes Trial, fundamentalists kept to themselves, focusing on evangelism, missions, and the ministry as opposed to sociopolitical concerns in the public arena. Fundamentalism rapidly became known for its stress on evangelism and its exclusion of actions in the sociopolitical arena.

During the half century following the Scopes Trial, liberal Protestants chided fundamentalists for their lack of sociopolitical involvement. By focusing only on "saving souls" they were considered to be neglecting a very important element of the Gospel—social *action* to relieve those suffering from social and political injustice, be it racism, poverty or a myriad of other social ills.

Mainstream Protestants castigated fundamentalists for abandoning social gospel efforts. It seemed that the assumption was made that if fundamentalists would again involve themselves sociopolitically, that they would be acting in accordance with mainstream social action efforts and assessments of the sources of social ills. Of course when fundamentalists did re-enter the socio-[ed: hypenated?] political arena with attempts to correct social ills as they perceived them, their actions were not in agreement with the perspectives of mainstream denominational Christians, much to the latter's dismay and disgust. Today fundamentalists are accused of "meddling" in politics (Yinger, et al., 1982:289). It is as if they have somehow lost their "right" to share in political concerns. Yinger and Cutler are quite fair in their statement that "the right of the Moral Majority to engage in politics is scarcely to be challenged, any more than is the right of critics to oppose them. The United States Constitution restricts the government somewhat ambiguously, of course, from establishing any religion or interfering with religious freedom; but no restrictions are placed on private individuals or the groups they organize. They are fully entitled to use their religious and ethical standards as criteria for selection in political matters."

Yinger and Cutler do not deny that Moral Majority spokesmen may be less tolerant, harsher or more certain of their exclusive hold on the truth than other, perhaps more liberal, religious groups involved in attempts to affect public policy, yet they understand that "disagreements over substance are made sharper by the addition of disagreements over method and style" (1982:290).

Why Now?

In the half century between the Scopes Trial and the establishment of the Moral Majority there were sporadic attempts, such as Billy James Hargis or Carl McIntyre to influence the sociopolitical realm, but not until the Moral Majority came on the scene in 1979 were there any long term successful attempts by purely fundamentalist groups to influence politics and to become a permanent power in society to be reckoned with. In fact this is one reason that fundamentalists and evangelicals split in the early forties: fundamentalists would not involve themselves in the sociopolitical arena. Though some fundamentalist denominations are members of the National Association of Evangelicals (established in 1942), the NAE is not limited to fundamentalist bodies and does not care to be identified with them, so we exclude them from our consideration of strictly fundamentalist social action organizations. Quebedeaux, in his book *The Young Evangelicals*, outlines some of the characteristics of evangelicals, and their characterization is clearly not in line with the characterization of fundamentalists outlined by Falwell in *The Fundamentalist Phenomenon*. Evangelicalism and fundamentalism are intertwined, but constitute distinct elements in American conservative Protestantism. Essentially, fundamentalism is often considered to be the right wing of the broader and larger evangelical movement.

Mainstream Protestants have not been too pleased with the social action efforts of right wing groups such as the Moral Majority, Religious Roundtable, Conservative Caucus, Christian Voice, National Christian Action Coalition, and others. Evangelical social action groups such as the Sojourners also have not been pleased with the far "right" activities and social stands. Today many Protestant liberals are wishing that this new breed of fundamentalist social activists would retreat to their previous stance of social and political inactivity where they were less of a nuisance.

Since 1979 the Moral Majority has been an influential fixture in American politics that defies its traditional fundamentalist roots. Now that the Moral Majority has played a role in two presidential elections, the question is being raised as to *why* fundamentalists are involved in social and political activism at this time in history.

There are many explanations for the rise of the religious right in the late seventies. Many popular explanations revolve around Hofstadter's (1966) and Gusfield's (1963) status politics argument. According to this theory a particular status group (defined by a common lifestyle) perceives a loss in its status and seeks to defend the lifestyle and regain status. Issues of moral concern are one way through which a cultural group acts to preserve, defend, or enhance the dominance and prestige of its own style of life.

> Besides their economic expectations, people have deep emotional commitments in other spheres—religion, morals, culture, race relations—in which they also hope to see realized in political action. Status politics seeks not to advance perceived material interests but to express grievances and resentments about such matters, to press claims upon society to give deference to non economic values. As a rule, status politics does more to express emotions than to formulate policies....The operative content of their demands is more likely to be negative; they call on us mainly to prohibit, to prevent, to censor and censure, to discredit, and to punish (Hofstadter, 1966:87-88).

Accordingly, people would be motivated to engage in public activism by a desire to defend a traditional lifestyle.

Then there's the "rise in social location" theory (cf. Harrell, 1981) which maintains that for the first time since the Scopes Trial fundamentalists sense that they have the resources, the power, and the ability to influence society. Harrell states:

> In short, the fundamentalist vanguard is not so much a frustrated middle-class which is losing control as it is an emerging middle-class flaunting its newly acquired respectability and power (1981:9).

In an interview with Greg Dixon, one of the founders of the Moral Majority and state chairman of Indiana's chapter of the Moral Majority until 1984, he stated that during the fundamentalist-modernist controversy the liberals "took over the denominations, capturing them for modernist beliefs." Dixon labeled this process "stealing." Accordingly, fundamentalists were "kicked out of the denominations and had to start from scratch in store front buildings on second-rate property while trying to hold on to the truths they held dear." If they were the poor and the uneducated who left the mainline denominations, it probably was due to the fact that they had less to lose by leaving the established denominations and more to gain by establishing suitable churches of their own. "As people began to wake up, they joined these new churches. These new works were based on Biblical Christianity. The reason it has taken so long to gain influence is because it took 50 to 60 years to rebuild churches, seminaries, colleges, orphanages, that had been taken over by the liberals. At the present, a constituency has been built up to fight back." (See Appendix A for transcript of interview.)

A third approach to the "why" of the New Right profile at this time in history, and an approach that is not inconsistent with the explanation cited above, is that promoted by Harrell and Marsden and it is simply this: "They have been provoked." Harrell explains that the virulent pro-Americanism of the religious right must be understood partly as a reaction to the virulent anti-Americanism that flourished in so many Christian agencies and seminaries in the 1960's and 1970's. As Peter Berger has noted, "Many American Christians felt they were faced with a choice between flag-burning and flag-waving" (Harrell, 1981:10). Harrell is quite correct when he says that "in the twentieth century, American conservative evangelicals have entered politics only when it seemed to them that the very structure of society was seriously threatened by modernism and liberalism" (1981:10).

Fundamentalism's deepest interests have always been religious, with occasional forays into politics on questions of personal morality. On two occasions in the twentieth century fundamentalists have felt compelled to launch crusades to save society; during the Scopes Trial and in the late seventies. Both periods of sociopolitical activity have been times when fundamentalists feared that the issues were the survival of Christian civilization. The evil that called for an all-out war effort in 1979 was secular humanism.[1]

Legitimations

Another question which must be addressed is how fundamentalist Christians rationalize their own political involvement in light of a previous stance of noninvolvement in political and social issues. Having used Biblical rationales to support their absence in social and political activism in decades past, how do they now legitimize their position reversal to support involvement in social activism?

This issue is illuminated if we take a look at their doctrinal stance involving premillennial-dispensationalism. In the late nineteenth century the premillenial-dispensational doctrine became widely accepted by American evangelicals. While originally outlined in the Scofield Reference Bible, it has been simplified and popularized by Hal Lindsey's *Late Great Planet Earth*. Accordingly, world history may be divided into seven "dispensations," the interruptions of this scheme by the church age, and the imminent beginning of a period of tribulation to be followed by the return of Christ and the beginning of the millennial reign of Christ on earth. The problem with premillennial-dispensationalism is that it clearly places history outside human manipulation and anticipates that change can come about only by cataclysmic supernatural intervention. Historically many people holding to this belief have been pessimistic and little given to political and social reform. Because they postulate that the world must become increasingly wicked until Christ returns to earth to set up His perfect Kingdom and millennial rule, many fundamentalists have a special problem with rationalizing why they should involve themselves with social ills at all.

The purpose of this book is to explore the issue of social activism within a group of people who, due to their theological and cultural orientation, would not be expected to engage in such behavior. As fundamentalist Christians, many members of the Moral Majority clearly remember being instructed from the pulpit to refrain

---

[1]Secular humanism is the name fundamentalists and others gave to the general philosophy behind the specific changes towards "liberalization" occurring in American society recently, i.e., abortion rights, sex education, women's rights, gay rights, anti-nuclear sentiment and others.

from social activism and encouraged to put their efforts into evangelism instead. Biblical rationales were used in this regard. In 1979 when Jerry Falwell and four fellow Baptist pastors founded the Moral Majority, Biblical rationales were also used to motivate followers to become activated for social concerns.[2] While fundamentalist clergy had little difficulty taking the leap from anti- to pro-social activism, many laypersons were bothered by this seeming contradiction and experienced serious cognitive dissonance over their ensuing involvement in social action concerns.

One only need to listen to a Jerry Falwell, Greg Dixon, Richard Viguerie or Paul Weyrich to understand why they feel compelled to engage in social activism. But how do lay members of the Moral Majority rationalize *their* participation in sociopolitical action? How do they differ from their pastors and Moral Majority leaders (often one and the same) in rationalizing social action concerns with the Gospel? As a relatively new religious right-wing social action organization, what kinds of social activism does the Moral Majority sponsor? Are Moral Majoritarians changing their cultural and religious assumptions in a way that would allow social activism a place of prominence heretofore frowned on by fundamentalists? And what about their doctrinal orientation which emphasizes a "rejoice when you see these evils in the world because this means the return of the Lord is near?" Does this spell out the rise of a new "plausibility structure" (to use Peter Berger's term), within which a new understanding of the world is adhered to?

To adequately address these issues, I have conducted in-depth interviews with several key leaders in the Moral Majority organization. I have also surveyed a scientific random sample of hundreds of members of the Moral Majority asking them to comment on these crucial issues. This cross-sectional data provides a wealth of information that helps to shed light on the issues of Moral Majority involvement *from the perspective of Moral Majoritarians* which is what makes this a rather unique contribution in the growing field of literature on the New Christian Right. I have not used secondary data, and I have not surveyed the general population at large to get ideas from nonmembers about Moral Majority

---

[2] These were the same arguments that the neo-evangelicals used in the 1940's.

involvement as other works have done. I have surveyed members of the Moral Majority itself to gather a composite picture of their attitudes, assumptions, social actions, theological views, and problems they are experiencing with their own involvement with social activism.

This book is divided into eight chapters which logically flow from the problems of fundamentalism and social activism. The first chapter deals with the roots of fundamentalism and the reasons they have eschewed social and political action since their beginnings with the fundamentalist-modernist controversy. The second chapter deals with the rise of the Moral Majority from within fundamentalism and the consequent involvement in social activism. The third chapter outlines my research method and measurement of variables. The fourth chapter deals with the issue of a new plausibility structure arising with the New Religious Right which now makes social and political activism a reasonable and acceptable behavioral alternative for Moral Majoritarians, especially among the clergy within the Moral Majority. Chapter Five relates to the relation of social location and its effect on social action. Chapter Six explores the relationship of social action behaviors and social action values for clergy and laity. Here is where we again see a major problem the laity have with social action behavior. Chapter Seven relates to the ensuing cognitive dissonance that this social action involvement has caused primarily for lay members of the Moral Majority. The eighth and final chapter deals with the prospects for change within the value system of the laity specifically. Since the laity are specifically the ones having most difficulty with their newfound involvement in social and political activism, they are the ones who will be most likely to undergo changes in the near future to a plausibility structure more accepting of social and political involvement.

I believe that this book makes a contribution to our understanding of the issues that surround what has been considered to be a social anomaly: that of organized fundamentalist involvement in social activism. Further, it is time for scholars to stop treating these newcomers to politics with suspicion and hostility. In the name of democracy, it is both appropriate and important to include them in dialogue. It may seem at first glance that New Right leaders are not amenable to dialogue. However, continued attacks from reputable writers and scholars will not enhance dialogue but may instead reinforce the "we against them" mentality and encourage counterattacks. The New Right has an obligation and legal right to participate in politics as well as the Old and New Left does. The First Amendment is applicable to all. If we believe the old dictum, "I may not agree with what you say, but I will fight to the death your right to say it," it's time we acknowledged the rights of opponents. Originally written as a doctoral dissertation, this work focuses on how Moral Majoritarians view their own involvement in social activism. One thing is clear: it is not trouble-free. I would like to express appreciation to James R. Wood who originally gave me direction in my thesis, David Knoke who gave me support and methodological guidance, Stephen Stein, John Simpson, Brian O'Connell and the late Nicholas Mullins for reviewing drafts of this work. Thanks goes to Mary La Tourelle who faithfully typed drafts, and Steve Robinson who gave editorial support. A special thanks goes to David and Amy Menges who with their computer expertise put the book in its final form. Thanks also goes to Seattle Pacific University for their support in this work. I take full responsibility for any errors or flaws contained herein.

Chapter One

Question: How integrated into society would you say that most Moral Majority members are?

Dixon: "They are on the periphery."

The Fundamentalist Movement

Long before the fundamentalist-modernist controversy developed in the first quarter of the twentieth century, social concern and evangelism tended to go hand-in-hand. Charles G. Finney, F. B. Meyer, John H. Jowett, Charles H. Spurgeon, and T. deWitt Talmadge were all eminent evangelical Christians of the past who were advocates of demonstrating one's faith in action.

The evangelicalism of the eighteenth century seemed to champion the causes of the weak. Prison reform, the prohibition of the slave trade, the Factory Acts, and the protection of children were the social expression of the great evangelical revival of the eighteenth century. These humanitarian tendencies continued among evangelicals into the nineteenth century. It wasn't until the twentieth century that fundamentalism arose within the mainline churches. When fundamentalists made their voices heard, it was generally in accordance with right-wing American politics. After the great depression, the stance they took was often one of fanatical opposition to the New Deal. Hofstadter (1966) notes that many right wing leaders of the depression and post-depression were preachers of fundamentalism. It seems that the pattern of fundamentalism within the conservative right has been the pattern of militant nationalism.

The fundamentalist movement of the early twentieth century was structured and identified as a reaction to the neglected theological affirmations of the mainline Protestant churches. As the modernist teachings of German higher criticism, Charles Darwin's theory of natural selection, and the Social Gospel increasingly became accepted in the mainline denominations, fundamentalists were provoked into making a fuss to uphold the biblical account of creation and a literal interpretation of Scripture. Reinhold Niebuhr has remarked that extreme orthodoxy "betrays by its very frenzy that the poison of skepticism has entered the soul of the church....Frantic orthodoxy is a method for obscuring doubt" (1927:2-3). A mix of dispensationalism and Princeton theology, fundamentalism originated as an intellectual movement in the metropolitan areas of the Northeast. The leadership was concentrated in urban centers, particularly in the Philadelphia-New York-Boston area, with lesser centers in Chicago, St. Louis and Los Angeles. The South was almost unrepresented until after the great depression (Sandeen, 1968: Marsden, 1980). Writers such as Stewart Cole and H. R. Niebuhr related the fundamentalist-modernist controversy to rural-urban conflict—between provincial small-town folk and sophisticated city dwellers.

Part of the cultural orientation that fundamentalism adopted and supported was a negative view of the world, pessimism toward the future, and anti-social-action values. In speaking of religion which limits its focus to purely spiritual concerns, Troeltsch (1931) notes that followers are indifferent, or impotent, towards all social problems which lie outside the directly religious sphere. Purely human activity is not really very meaningful. Legislative action, for example, can never produce morals or right thinking. Only the Spirit of God can furnish the power by which these dispositions can be accomplished. Fundamentalists were even more deeply convinced that human thinking and acting were on an irretrievable downgrade which humans were powerless to reverse and which was one of the clearest signs of the imminence of the second advent of Christ. Premillennial-dispensationalists believe that there will be no true theocracy or theonomy until Christ returns to earth. So they are relieved of the unnecessary and heavy burden postmillennarians[1] have placed on themselves to bring in the kingdom (Geisler, 1985).

---

[1]Postmillennarians, of which there are few in fundamentalist or evangelical circles, believe that the church is obligated to usher in the kingdom. They believe that the future kingdom (millennium) is to be brought about by forces now active in the world. It is understandable then that their view manifests the closest relationship between church and state, and between God and government. Premillennarians hold to a discontinuity between the present dispensation and the

Fundamentalist Doctrine

The division of world history into seven dispensations involving a "tribulation" period followed by the return of Christ and His millennial reign is part of the doctrinal stance of premillennial-dispensationalism. This complex belief system affected practically all Protestant denominations at the start of the twentieth century, and its popularity was due in large part to the appearance of the Scofield Reference Bible (1909) which imposed a rigid timetable on the various *dispensations* found in the Bible where God is seen to relate differently to man. Consistent with Scofield's scheme was the idea that the established denominations had become apostate and true Christians should separate from ecclesiastical bodies. Dispensationalism took prophetic portions of Scripture literally and branded theological liberalism as Satanic (Quebedeaux, 1974:8).

However, the roots of premillennialism go back to the first century.[2] In fact the Gnostics were the first to reject the premillennial view. They were followed by Caius, Origen, and Dionysius, all of whom engaged in allegorical interpretation of the Bible (Geisler, 1985:251). Eusebius recorded the millennial beliefs of Cerinthus saying that he believed that "after the resurrection there would be an earthly kingdom of Christ."[3] Of Papias, Eusebius wrote, "He says there would be a certain millennium after the resurrection and that there would be a corporeal reign of Christ on this very earth."[4]

Justin Martyr declared, "I and others,...are assured that there will be a resurrection of the dead, and a thousand years in Jerusalem, which will then be built, adorned, and enlarged, [as] the prophets Ezekiel and Isaiah and others

---

future kingdom. Only Christ can inaugurate the millennium. Therefore, they manifest less identity between the kingdom of God and civil politics (Geisler, 1985:250).

[2]"Among earlier writers the belief was held by authors of Epistle of Barnabas [4,15], the Shepherd, the Second Epistle of Clement, by Papias, Justin, and by some of the Ebionites, and Cerinthus....The premillennial view was also shared by Irenaeus, Melito, Hippolytus, Tertullian, and Lactantius." Quoted in Geisler (1985:251).

[3]Eusebius Pamphilus, *Ecclesiastical History of Eusebius Pamphilus* (Grand Rapids: Baker Book House, 1955), p. 113.

[4]Ibid., p. 126.

declare."[5] Tertullian wrote, "We confess that a kingdom is promised to us upon earth, only in another state of existence; inasmuch as it will be after the resurrection for a thousand years in the divinely built city of Jerusalem."[6]

The premillennial view continued strong until the fourth century when it was first embraced by Augustine. He later gave it up but never undertook to refute the premillennial view (Geisler, 1985:251). He even conceded that it would not be objectionable as long as premillinarians did not "assert that those who then rise again shall enjoy the leisure of immoderate carnal banquets."[7]

Augustine's reaction to premillennialism prevailed in medieval Roman Catholicism up to the Reformation, in which the primary concern was with soteriology, not eschatology. During the Reformation the premillennial view was strongly represented by the Swiss brethren such as Conrad Grebel, Felix Manz, and George Blawrock. The Dutch Anabaptist, Meno Simmons (d. 1561), was also premillennial. The German Calvinist, Johann Heinrich Alsted (1588-1638), returned to the premillennial view of the early church fathers in his book *The Beloved City* (1627), which caused the learned Anglican scholar, Joseph Mede (1586-1638), to become a premillenarian. In America the millennial position was forwarded by Cotton Mather (1691) who held that "there will be a time when Jerusalem shall be literally rebuilt, and people all over the world shall be under the influence of that Holy City."[8]

Jonathan Edwards (1637-1716) believed in six dispensations and a thousand-year reign of Christ, albeit a spiritual one. Isaac Watts (1674-1748), who was not only premillennial but also a forerunner of dispensationalism, outlined six dispensations plus a millennium which correspond exactly to those of the Scofield Bible.[9]

---

[5]Justin Martyr Dialogue with Trypho (*The Ante-Nicene Fathers*, ed. Alexander Roberts and James Donaldson, 9 vols. [Grand Rapids: Wm. B. Eerdmans Pub. Co., 1977] 1:239).

[6]Tertullion, *Against Marcion* (The Ante-Nicene Fathers, 3:342).

[7]Augustine, *City of God* (The Nicene and Post-Nicene Fathers), ed. Philip Schaff, 14 vols. Grand Rapids: Wm. B. Eerdmans Pub. Co., 1956, 2:426.

[8]Quoted in Geisler (1985:266). Cotton Mather, *Things to Be Look'd For* (New England:n. p., 1691), 1.4.

[9]Isaac Watts, *The Works of the Rev. Isaac Watts, D.D.*, 7 vols. (Leeds: Edward Baines, n.d.) 2:625.

Johann H. Bengel, Isaac Newton and Joseph Priestly carried on the premillennial view in the eighteenth century. In the nineteenth century Edward Irving of the Church of Scotland fostered a widespread interest in premillennialism. The latter part of the nineteenth century witnessed a full-blown form of dispensational premillennialism in the writings of John Nelson Darby (1800-1882).[10]

At the turn of the century, C. I. Scofield, through the Scofield Reference Bible, had a wide influence on American premillennialism (Geisler, 1985:252). Because of the theological implications of premillennialism some have urged believers "not to polish the brass rails on the sinking social ship." Instead, they urge Christians to focus on "saving souls." As mentioned, premillennialist fundamentalists were originally deeply involved in social matters in their origins. A. C. Dixon, who edited *The Fundamentals* (1910-1915), went so far as to encourage Christians to organize political parties (Geisler, 1985:254). But this was before the Scopes Trial. And today, Jerry Falwell, Timothy LaHaye[11] and Pat Robertson are pushing for social involvement.

"While premillennialists believe that there will be no true theocracy or theonomy until Christ returns to earth, postmillennialists believe that they must Christianize the world. Hence they are infected with the optimism that eventually 'evil in all its many forms will be reduced to negligible proportions' and 'the race, as a race, will be saved.'"[12]   This would seem to imply that postmillennialists would assume the extraordinary burden of Christianizing the world and establishing God's rule on earth. Ironically, missions' handbooks seem to indicate that it is the premillennialist portion of Christendom which may be carrying the lion's share of evangelism (cf. Geisler, 1985:256).

Around the same time that the Scofield Reference Bible was published, Amzi Dixon (1854-1925) and Reuben Archer Torey (1856-1928) edited ten small volumes entitled the "fundamentals of faith." The five "fundamentals" were

---

[10]John Darby, *The Collected Writings of J. N. Darby*, ed. William Kelly, 34 vols. (reprint, Sunburg, PA: Believers Bookshelf, 1971) 2:568.73.

[11]The Rev. Timothy La Haye is a co-founder of the Moral Majority and a co-founder of the Institute for Creation Research in San Diego.

[12]Boettner, "Postmillennialism," pp. 118, 123.

identified as: (1) the verbal inspiration of the Bible, (2) the virgin birth of Christ, (3) His substitutionary atonement, (4) His bodily resurrection, and (5) His imminent and visible Second Coming. Three million copies had been distributed and paid for by two Los Angeles millionaires, Milton and Lyman Stewart.

While both fundamentalists and evangelicals give assent to the "five fundamentals," fundamentalism differs from evangelicalism in its basic attitudes. The fundamentalist stance seems to embrace "the quest for negative status, the elevation of minor issues to a place of major importance, the use of social mores as a norm of virtue and the toleration of one's own prejudices, but not the prejudices of others, the confusion of the church with a denomination, and the avoidance of prophetic scrutiny by using the Word of God as a instrument of self-security but not self-criticism" (Carnell, 1969:169-70). Fundamentalists also differ from evangelicals in their nonacceptance of Pentecostals and charismatics. Evangelicals have accepted Pentecostals and charismatics into their community of fellowship. In fact, Thomas Zimmerman, past General Superintendent of the Assemblies of God, has served as Executive Director of the National Association of Evangelicals.

The fundamentalists of the twenties were considered to be the disenfranchised, the embarrassing element to the mainline churches which were growing increasingly sophisticated and liberal in their beliefs. Fundamentalists believed they were deliberately excluded from and despised by the leadership elites in American life. Some scholars are now defending the fundamentalist contention that they *have* indeed been excluded and despised. Neuhaus (1982), for example, maintains that fundamentalist religion was excluded from respectable circles and made an object of ridicule in the 1920's. Today fundamentalists are still an object of ridicule among mainline denominations.

Edward John Carnell maintains that fundamentalism tends to draw followers from two sources: (1) those who are "separatists" by nature and who have little if any concern for the church universal, and (2) those whose theological and cultural attitudes have been shaped almost exclusively by the negativism of the fundamentalist-modernist controversy.[13]

---

[13] The fundamentalist-modernist controversy involved the dispute over Darwinism—a dispute that has not been settled even today. See *Time*, November 1986.

Richard Quebedeaux identified two subgroups within fundamentalism. There are separatist fundamentalists and open fundamentalists. Separatist fundamentalists are the direct descendants of groups who took part in the fundamentalist-modernist controversy. These are those who felt it necessary to separate completely from any manifestation of liberalism or modernism. It is difficult to distinguish their theological concerns from their professed social and political stance. The most cherished doctrines of separatist fundamentalism are (1) total separation from ungodliness—especially as manifested in liberalism and evangelicalism, (2) the verbal inspiration and inerrancy of the Bible, and (3) premillennial (and generally dispensational) apocalypticism (Quebedeaux, 1974:20).[14]

Due in large part to dispensational theology, separatist fundamentalism holds to an extremely pessimistic view of the present world situation. Society is seen to be rapidly decaying with apostasy becoming rampant in the church. Separatist fundamentalism looks forward to (1) the immanent rapture of the church (the "saved" being lifted into the skies to meet Christ and thence to heaven), followed in succession by (2) the earthly rule of Antichrist during the seven-year Great Tribulation, (3) the battle of Armageddon, (4) the millennial reign of Christ on earth, (5) another brief time of woes and Satan's rule over the world, and finally, the Great White Throne Judgment in which the Devil and the damned are cast into the lake of everlasting and literal fire, while the righteous are rewarded by eternal bliss in heaven that includes only separatist fundamentalists (Quebedeaux, 1974:21).

> This 'rapture' means the instantaneous pretribulation 'catching up' of the righteous, a remarkable event which any day now will empty assorted fundamentalist churches and leave cars with appropriate bumper stickers driverless, while at the same time leaving untouched the entire faculty and student body of Yale Divinity School.(Harrell, 7).

---

[14]Falwell's definition of "separation" is somewhat different. In an interview with *Christianity Today* he said, "For me, the definition of separation from the world may be different from some others. I don't use alcoholic beverages and I preach teetotalism. That would be the practice of 18,000 members of this church. I don't think it has anything to do with salvation. But when I talk about separation, I mean separation from the rock music culture, separation from immorality, separation from the Hollywood culture."

In the context of dispensational ideology, one can understand why involvement in politics is seen to be a losing battle. Only Christ's return can stay the tide against Satan. It invites retreat from the world, not hand-to-hand combat with the minions of Satan (Hadden, 1985:25). The Last Days must increase in decadence until the "rapture" at which time the "saved" will be removed from the sinful world. It is interesting to note, however, that separatist fundamentalists continue to fight for the status quo, the Protestant ethic and American militarism (Quebedeaux, 1974:22).

Hal Lindsey, in *The Late Great Planet Earth*, outlines the "end times." The "last days" scenario goes like this: According to Apostle John in the book of Revelation, a force from the east will wipe out one-third of the world's population. Among the Jews who survive this Armageddon, many will be converted to Jesus as their true Messiah. When the "great war" reaches such a pitch that it seems that no life will be left on earth, Jesus will return and save humankind from total self-extinction by preserving the faithful remnant. McGuire (1982) feels that :

> ...rightists need a war, just as they needed the foundation of Israel. Nuclear war squares nicely with some of the Scriptural language about the fiery tribulation that will inaugurate the latter days—the big chastening blast that will set the stage for Jesus's triumphant return....The millennial hope induces a pious nonchalance in New Right believers. The coming inaugural will do them no harm. True believers can view this impending judgment with a...calm. Their faith is their thermonuclear insurance. They will be saved by a blessed 'rapture,' lifted up to meet Christ 'in the air,' while the good earth and unbelievers are scorched in the final holocaust (McGuire, 1982:18).

This is one reason why non-fundamentalists who are aware of fundamentalist theology are terrified to have a fundamentalist president or fundamentalist power coalition in Washington, D.C. If the end is coming, and by end we mean the destruction of the world as we know it, there is a question as to what motivation a fundamentalist would have to attempt a redirection of history? Why cooperate with the Soviet Union? Jerry Falwell has despised the SALT talks and thinks we are too soft with the Soviet Regime.

While we may want to acknowledge that all Americans have the right to enter the political process, the question is often asked what the end result would be *if* a candidate such as a Pat Robertson[15] were to become president, or if fundamentalists gained control of Congress? While many fundamentalists believe that liberal democrats might give the nation away without a fight rather than stand up for moral values, many centrists as well as leftists fear that a fundamentalist might be anxious to lead America into the battle of Armageddon since fundamentalist theology anticipates it.

If one looked simply at the implications of fundamentalist theology, it might seem logical that fundamentalists should be pacifistic in relation to military war instead of "hawkish." If the end time is set according to pattern, why fight the natural course of history? If a Communist takeover is inevitable, what difference would it make? It would serve to hurry the coming of Christ and the rapture. According to dispensationalism, the born-again Christian would have little to worry about, as the will of God would be done in any case. However, fundamentalists tend to be in favor of military buildup, and are not commonly labelled as "doves."

The premillennial dispensationalism of separatist fundamentalism is marked by its rejection of the present age and world and any attempt to bring change. It usually leads to social passivity. Quebedeaux (1974) puts it quite strongly:

> Separatist fundamentalism, with its dispensational pessimism about the human situation, its firm commitment to the political and social status quo, its anti-intellectualism heightened by an inherent refusal to be self-critical or to compromise, and its ideology of separatistism is totally destitute of a social conscience.

While a common response to premillennialism is involvement in evangelism and the avoidance of social activism, some fundamentalists take literally the Scriptural admonition to "...rejoice when you see these things happening...because thereby shall you know that your redemption draweth nigh." "Evil men and seducers shall wax worse and worse, deceiving and being deceived" (II Tim. 3:13). Because their eschatological interpretation of history is one of progressive degeneration, deterioration, and devolution until the establishment of Christ's

---

[15]As Pentecostal, Pat Robertson does not fit into the fundamentalist camp. However, the theological formulation, excluding the Pentecostal doctrine of speaking in tongues, does fit the fundamentalist model.

millennial kingdom, the worse things get, the closer His coming must be, so they rejoice (cf. Moberg, 1972:21).

While there has been no social ethic in separatist fundamentalism historically, with respect to personal ethics, negativism prevails. They disapprove of drinking, smoking, social dancing, gambling, and attendance at the theater. Righteous external behavior is emphasized. "Ethics has nothing to do with how a committed Christian treats other people as persons created in the image of God and for whom Christ died. And human love—not to mention Christ's love—appears to have no real importance in that school of thought" (Quebedeaux, 1974:22). The focus is on individualistic acts, not relations.

Open fundamentalism is less clearly defined than separatist fundamentalism. It is much like separatist fundamentalism except that it repudiates the explicit alliance of fundamentalism with ultraconservative politics. They believe that religious and political spheres ought to be separate. However, open fundamentalism tends to support the conservative and anticommunist position on most social and political issues. Like separatist fundamentalism, it holds to a basic separatism from the historic denominations and their "unbelieving" theologians and ministers. But open fundamentalism is less vocal and less extreme about its posture. It is not inherently anti-intellectual and is often willing to engage in dialogue with other Orthodox schools of thought. It is also capable of some degree of self-criticism (Quebedeaux, 1974:26).

Open fundamentalism could be understood as a rough equivalent to a definition of evangelicalism. By and large, evangelicals disdain being lumped together with fundamentalists in the mind of mainstream liberals but, at times, fundamentalists do not mind being labelled with the more respectable term evangelical. However, most fundamentalist leaders are proud to be called "fundamentalists." Jerry Falwell and Greg Dixon have made it clear in the past that they have been proud to be counted as such. However, Jerry Nims, current President of the Moral Majority, identifies himself as a "mainline evangelical," and Jerry Falwell himself has been embracing the term evangelical as of late. This is somewhat surprising in light of earlier statements.

What is the difference between today's fundamentalist and the proto-fundamentalists of the nineteenth century? The latter were frequently men held in high esteem in their own denominations and communities. By 1900 fundamentalism (though not yet called such) was a significant force in American life emphasizing evangelism and world missions. It was not until the controversies of the 1920's that clangor and strife turned fundamentalism into a term of reproach for some people.[16] Hofstadter (1966) is sympathetic to fundamentalists for their attempt to save the family pieties from the ravages of evolutionists, intellectuals, and cosmopolitans (1966:126).

Fundamentalism did not get its name until the twenties when fundamentalist organizations were mobilizing. The early intellectual fathers had died out by the time of the Scopes Trial when the press seized upon William Jennings Bryan, who was not a fundamentalist,[17] as the "spokesman for a numerically large segment of people who (were) for the most part inarticulate." The Darwinian controversy remained the focal point for the controversy between fundamentalists and modernists beginning with the Scopes Trial.

The Scopes Trial

The State of Tennessee passed a bill to prevent the teaching of evolution in the public schools. Shortly thereafter in a drugstore a few people opposing the law agreed that substitute biology teacher, John Thomas Scopes, should be brought to trial to test this "foolish law." Scopes agreed to be arrested, though he wasn't sure he actually had taught evolution. The American Civil Liberties Union had offered to defend any teacher who was prosecuted under it. William Jennings Bryan said he would represent the World Christian Fundamentals Association without charge. Bryan had not been in a courtroom in twenty-eight years (Szasz, 1982:117).

---

[16]The term "fundamentalist" as applied to a particular group of people within American Protestantism is of relatively recent origin, the first outstanding usage being in 1909 with the publishing of "The Fundamentals," and the first specific designation of the term being made by the editor of the Watchman-Examiner in 1920. Everett L. Perry, (1959).

[17]Contrary to popular opinion, Bryan was not a premillennialist or a fundamentalist of any type. His philosophy and the anti-evolution crusade was incompatible with the assumptions of millennarianism. See Szasz, pp. 110-111.

Though fundamentalists won the case, they were noted for their general divisiveness and discord. It seemed that when they were not fighting modernists or liberals, they were fighting with Roman Catholics. And when not fighting Roman Catholics, they seemed to be fighting each other. Jerry Falwell (1981) has stated that if there isn't anything to fight about, fundamentalist's are likely to start a fight. From the time of the Scopes Trial, fundamentalism was popularly linked with anti-intellectualism, bad manners, and obscurantism.

During the trial, Clarence Darrow mentioned that "every child ought to be more intelligent than his parents." Here he frightened fundamentalists as this was exactly what they did not want. If being more intelligent meant that children were expected to abandon parental ideas and desert their ways, they could do without it. Bryan made the statement that "our only purpose is to vindicate the right of parents to guard the religion of their children..." (Hofstadter, 1966:127). This is the same cry of Greg Dixon's[18] organization, "National Coalition of Unregistered Churches," a loosely organized network with a goal of providing educational materials on Constitutional Rights and Biblical principles for "churches in trouble."[19] Secular education has always been a threat to fundamentalists, and parental responsibility to oversee their children's education has been one of the primary battle cries.

The trial exemplified the polarization of Protestantism in the 1920's and many saw the trial in terms of the fight between cognitive domains of authority: between skepticism and faith. The trial portrayed the fundamentalist idea of democracy: that ultimate decisions must always be determined by the people. This attitude shows up again among members of the Moral Majority who claim— perhaps rightly so—that the American people agree with them on the issues. The

---

[18]Greg Dixon, pastor of Baptist Temple, an 8000-member Independent Baptist Church in Indianapolis, is co-founder of the Moral Majority and past Chairman of the Indiana Chapter of the Moral Majority. He resigned his position with the Moral Majority in 1983 to head up the "Coalition of Independent Churches" to fight for church rights. Dixon came to national attention when he led 400 ministers who formed a human chain around Reverend Lester Roloff's home for children to prevent its closing by Texas welfare officials. During the 1970's Dixon also organized large rallies in support of Anita Bryant's anti-homosexuality campaign, the Church Freedom Legislative Package, and strict controls on pornography (*Conservative Digest*, August 1979).

[19]Holladay, Ruth, "Greg Dixon: Preaching Resistance puts Church at Odds with State." *The Indianapolis Star*, Sunday, December 29, 1985.

implication is that this should be sufficient rationale to change public policy on issues.

After the depression, fundamentalist organizations began to grow. The intellectual leadership that had characterized the movement in its earliest days had long since dissipated. The newer, younger leadership did not always have the intellectual and social stature of those they replaced. Itinerant preachers and revivalists came on the scene converting those who were either suffering from denominational neglect or who felt uncomfortable in the more sophisticated mainline churches. The pessimistic attitude of fundamentalists toward social problems, the future, and society often attracted inferior classes of people and intensified their tendency toward human fatalism. Some have related the cultural lag of fundamentalists in the scholastic realm to their premillennialistic beliefs. Others held that the radical orthodoxy, biblical literalness and rigid Protestant morality of fundamentalism were a line of defense to a way of life that was losing its dominance. The increase of large-scale industry, rapid urban growth and the influx of immigrants were causing evangelical Protestantism to suffer. The fundamentalist movement was often interpreted to be a "backlash" reaction to the loss of evangelical strength in the nation (Niebuhr, 1932). American society was becoming cosmopolitan, secular and metropolitan. By 1920 urban dwellers were in the majority for the first time in American history (Lipsett and Raab, 1970).

Those who joined the established fundamentalist movement in the twenties were those who professed beliefs in the supernatural elements of the Christian faith. This group integrated their anomic experiences and outcast status into a socially established worldview. The certainty of their socially established "nomos" was "dredged up" from within their subjective consciousness. It was not derived from the external, socially shared and taken-for-granted world of society at large (cf. Berger, 1967). Sandeen (1970) writes that the roots of fundamentalism have to do with the Calvinist orthodoxy of Princeton Seminary and millenarians. Marsden (1980:4) views fundamentalist roots as coming from numerous other traditions, including evangelicalism, revivalism, pietism, the Holiness movement, premillennialism, Reformed confessionalism, Baptist traditionalism and other denominational orthodoxies. However one wishes to understand the roots of fundamentalism, the Bible and religious beliefs played an important part in shaping the movement.

Meredith McGuire (1982) notes that when groups cannot partake in the widely accepted social world of society at large, they often devise sub-societal plausibility structures to provide the answers to their particular problem of meaning. This appears to be what the fundamentalist movement did for many who rejected the increasingly urban, scientific, and secular views of the mainline churches and society at large. Contained in the fundamentalist outlook (as in all orthodox Christianity) is the view that all men were corrupted by sin and needed a special supernatural rescue. Mankind needed to be redeemed and only through spiritual regeneration could society hope to be transformed. Therefore sociopolitical activism with the aim of reconstructing society was considered to be worthless effort without consideration for the Creator-Redeemer God and His holy commandments. Though there is a growing movement among many fundamentalists to "reconstruct society" according to biblical principles, this was not an issue in the earlier days of the fundamentalist movement.

A result of fundamentalism's concentration on spiritual concerns was that it gave them one area in which they could excel and demonstrate superiority over those disagreeing with their interpretation of Scripture and worldview. They could be rich in spiritual knowledge and standards—richness which secular society did not have. But in terms of earthly wealth such as material goods, education or prestigious occupations, fundamentalists were often poor. Consequently, earthly possessions were given little value and even were thought to be a hindrance toward achieving spiritual gain in this life or rewards in the hereafter. Lipset (1970) notes that "low status backlash movements oftentimes invoke aggressively moralistic stances because the moral superiority of one group over another in the end is all that may be invoked."

Fundamentalists did perform a modicum of social action in the late nineteenth and early part of the twentieth centuries. But as the fundamentalist-modernist controversy developed and raged and the mainline churches were seen to be dispensing with the supernatural elements of Christianity, fundamentalists took on more of an evangelistic zeal and reactionary thrust to uphold the fundamentals of the faith. The fundamentalist movement of the twentieth century may be interpreted as a conservative response to the spread of theological liberalism.

After William Jennings Bryan there was Billy James Hargis, Carl McIntire and others who contributed to reinforcing the stereotypes that Sinclair Lewis and H. L. Mencken delighted in promoting. All of these individuals attracted followings but none ever managed to develop sufficient resources to seriously challenge any major aspect of American life. "Thus while they represent surviving residuals of the movement, we can conclude that the fundamentalist social movement, which had gained considerable strength during the first half of the 1920's, lost its momentum and then fizzled after 1925" (Hadden, 1985:18). Edward John Carnell, past president of Fuller Theological Seminary, has reportedly said, in effect, that fundamentalism's distinctiveness is found in its attempt to

> ...maintain its own house by the negation of others. When fundamentalism started dwelling on the negative, it changed from a religious movement to a religious mentality. It never developed an affirmative world view and made no effort to connect its convictions to the wider problems of society....Fundamentalism is a lonely position. It has cut itself off from the general stream of culture, philosophy, ecclesiastical tradition. This accounts, in part, for its robust pride. Since it is no longer in union with the wisdom of the ages, it has no standard by which to judge its own religious pretense. It dismisses non-fundamentalistic efforts as empty, futile, or apostate. Its tests for Christian fellowship become so severe that divisions in the church are considered a sign of virtue. And when there are no modernists from which to withdraw, fundamentalists compensate by withdrawing from one another (quoted in Hadden & Swann, 1981:86-87).

Fundamentalism was instrumental in the cultural backlash of the twenties mainly because it was the prime cultural property of those whose understanding of the world was being threatened (Lipset and Raab, 1970). A large part of the fundamentalist agitation resulted from the fear that fundamentalists would no longer be able to preach the Christ and worldview that they knew and were accustomed to (cf. Harrell, 1981; and Marsden, 1980). As with most people, fundamentalists like to feel that they have a comprehensive world view, and their minds are more satisfied when religious and political antipathies can be linked together. They have developed a gift for combining seemingly irrelevant animosities so as to make them mutually reinforcing (Hofstadter, 1966:133).

The fundamentalist movement had affected practically all of the denominations except perhaps the Unitarians and Congregationalists. It severely disrupted the Northern Baptists and Northern Presbyterians and reaffirmed long-standing divisions within the Disciples, Episcopalians, and Northern and Southern Methodists. Until the late twenties, fundamentalism was not so much a denominational issue as it was a liberal/conservative issue irrespective of denominational affiliation. By the time of the great depression the popular mind considered newfound conservative groups such as the Seventh Day Adventists, Pentecostals, Nazarenes and Baptist sects to be fundamentalist organizations (cf. Szasz, 1982), though not all of them were.

Opposition to an educational elite was a major part of fundamentalism in the twenties and continues to be so in the eighties. Szasz views fundamentalism as the last revolt of the average man, the person who believed that nothing was beyond his grasp. The fundamentalist's complete confidence in ordinary people carried with it a distrust of those who were exceptional, a scorn for advanced learning, and often for scholarship in general. This helps to account for the fundamentalist reputation of being anti-intellectual.

Evangelicalism and Fundamentalism

There is much confusion as to what constitutes evangelicalism and fundamentalism. To a theological liberal or non-Christian they are often confused and seen to be one and the same entity as evidenced by much media coverage. But many committed evangelicals are often painfully aware of the differences. Fundamentalism is the right edge of the broader and larger evangelical movement which has grown by millions of adherents in the past two decades. Though they oftentimes are loosely categorized together, (Pierard, 1983), there are distinct differences.

In looking at some major differences between theological liberalism, evangelicalism, and fundamentalism, Richard Quebedeaux (1974) notes that:

Evangelicalism transcends denominations and their respective polities...and it can well be termed an ideologically conservative *movement* rather than a church or denomination. Evangelicalism is conservative insofar as it differs from liberalism, which either denies or bypasses the three basic theological principles [which] evangelicalism affirms.

The three basic theological principles being referred to are (1) the complete reliability and final authority of Scripture in matters of faith and practice; (2) the necessity of a personal faith in Jesus Christ as Savior from sin and consequent commitment to Him as Lord; and (3) the urgency of seeking actively the conversion of sinners to Christ.

Though some scholars such as George Marsden and Carl Henry would treat fundamentalism and evangelicalism together, others such as Hofstadter and Richard Quebedeaux treat them as being significantly different.

It has often been said that a fundamentalist is an angry evangelical. This is probably because cultural fundamentalists are adamant in their beliefs, and tend to reject cultural change. They favor tradition because it is tradition. They are not tolerant of new ideas and tend to reject new values such as those related to the social ethic centering on self-fulfillment (cf. Yankelovich, 1981).

When Jerry Falwell was asked how he would define a fundamentalist, he replied that a fundamentalist is "one who first, believes in the inerrancy of Scriptures and second, is committed to biblical separation in the world and to the Lordship of Christ" (*Christianity Today*, September 4, 1981). Scholars such as Lipset and Raab (1982) have found no statistical difference between evangelicals and non-evangelicals on attitudes towards a number of issues. They concluded from Gallup figures that the term "evangelical" was meaningless when interpreting reactions to general political issues. However, Patel, Pilant and Rose (1982) found significant differences in attitudes toward public policy issues between "born-again" and "not born-again" people. Theological self designation is considered by many to be the most powerful explanatory variable (i.e., Harper & Leight, 1983). Being "born-again" of course is a fundamentalist (and an evangelical) trademark. Patel et al. found that 80% of born-again Christians in their sample favored a constitutional amendment to permit prayer and Bible reading in public school whereas 60% of not born-again respondents favored it (Patel et al.). And they found that while both born-again and non-born-again respondents felt that books with "bad words" should be removed from public libraries, 39% of born-again respondents opposed the move and 22% of non-born-again respondents opposed the move.

The Apocalyptic World View
(Premillennialist)

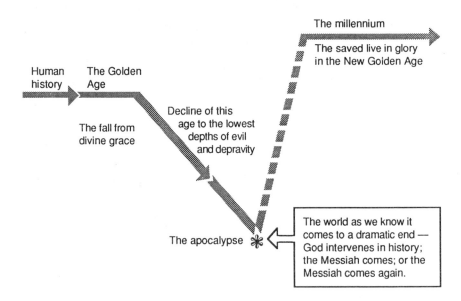

Daniel and Revelation present a consistent apocalyptic worldview in the Bible. Daniel was written when the Hebrew people were under the most severe oppression and felt powerless and vulnerable. Likewise, the Book of Revelation was written at a time in the Roman Empire when one could be put to death for being a Christian. But despite the fact that apocalypticism is atypical in the Bible, many Christian sects (including fundamentalists) sustain a worldview based primarily on the outlook of those two apocalyptic books. In most cases, this view is adopted by those whose social circumstance makes them feel powerless and vulnerable.

(Taken from Keith A. Roberts, *Religion in Sociological Perspective* [Homewood, Ill.: Dorsey Press], p. 308-9.)

Cultural Fundamentalism

Values, roles and cultural practices supported by fundamentalists were thought to be derived from Scripture, but might also have stemmed from their position in society. Ideological justification has often been noted to follow the engagement of social practices (cf. Lipset and Raab). In this sense the intense spiritual values supported by fundamentalism might have resulted from the limited subculture of a class of people who had little social influence or power. This does not mean that they did not believe their doctrinal tenets or spiritual values. However, the cultural practices emanating from their spiritual values and doctrinal beliefs were related to their position—or lack of it—in society.

Fundamentalism's inability to accept the growing sophistication and liberalizing of the mainline churches, and the inability of the wealthy and prestigious church bodies to provide meaning and comfort to the lower classes (cf. Kelley, 1972) contributed to the lower classes forming their own fundamentalist sects to provide a suitable expression for their religiosity. Against the liberal theologies of immanence and social gospel, fundamentalists stressed God's transcendent and suprahistorical power and expressed themselves in pessimistic terms when discussing social problems. The social gospel of the liberals was no gospel at all to the fundamentalists, who saw in the Bible only a gospel for saving individuals, not one for redeeming the social order (Chafer, *Systematic Theology*, 7:177). The fundamentalist attitude reflected a distrust of reason and more of an emphasis upon intuition and emotion. Human ability was incapable of solving ultimate problems. Humanity needed the guidance of divine agency. H. Richard Niebuhr (1929) notes that these characteristics are typical of groups who have received the least profit from a rationalized culture.

There has always been a great divide between those who understand salvation in essentially private or essentially public terms. In the privatized version, typical of fundamentalists, salvation is essentially a matter of personal redemption resulting in one's getting his or her soul into heaven, while the rest of the reality we call history can, quite literally, go to hell. The world is already condemned and the only relevant question is, "Are you saved?" More liberal Christians insist that the Gospel must have public significance and that it must illuminate human experience within the political realm. It has therefore been judged that fundamentalism, with its focus on privatized salvation, is indifferent to political involvement, while liberal Christianity takes politics seriously but shortchanges the need for personal salvation (cf. Neuhaus, 1984:14).

The fundamentalist cultural orientation is supported by complex legitimations which defend it when confronted with opposing views. Gusfield (1963) coined the term "cultural fundamentalist" referring to, among other things, those who assert older, traditional values which have been identified with the old middle class of the nineteenth century. "Cultural modernists" identify the modern as the normative order to be followed. Although the cultural fundamentalist is identified with rural doctrines, he is found in both city and country. The stance is inward, toward one's immediate environment and immediate mediating structures like family and church. The cultural modernist looks outward, to the media of mass communications, the national organizations, the colleges and universities, and the influences which originate outside of his local community. The modernist reveres the future and change as good; the fundamentalist reveres the past and sees change as damaging and upsetting (1963:140). Here we can get a glimpse as to why New Right groups such as the Moral Majority do not fit well into the cultural fundamentalist framework of Gusfield's.

There are two types of fundamentalist reaction to social change: one defensive and one aggressive. The defensive reaction involves a preoccupation with the regeneration of values in many areas—family life, child training, and religion. Here, American life is depicted as having degenerated from an earlier position of virtue, authority, morality, and respect for age. There is a sense of estrangement from the dominant values and the belief that a return of the dominant values of the past, based on good old-fashioned religion, will solve social problems as evidenced in the drug scene, homosexual and illicit sexual illnesses, and even racism and poverty. "It is not uncommon to hear in fundamentalist churches that

America is as degraded as Rome was before its fall...there is a complete moral and spiritual degradation" (Gusfield, 1963:144).

On the aggressive reactionary side, hostility is directed toward modernity for declining middle class values. Human society, psychiatry, modern child rearing, contemporary educational practices are among those institutions attacked as immoral, responsible for present-day ills. Schools, entertainment and even major churches are seen as the source for decay of traditional values.

The modern issue that the New Right is wrestling with concerns whose culture (modern/traditional or Judeo-Christian/Anti-Judeo-Christian) is to be granted legitimacy by the public action of government (cf. Gusfield, 1963:148).

For example, one legitimation given for the failure of fundamentalists to engage in social action is that the world is lost or doomed. According to the premillenialist view of history, the world belongs to the kingdom of Satan and has been lost since the Fall of man. Luke 4:5-6 is taken to mean that the governments of this world system (cf. Matt. 4:8-9) are under Satan's authority.[20] The present dispensation will contain good and bad, wheat and tares, until Christ comes (Geisler, 1985:259). Evangelism, therefore, has received legitimation whereas social action has been discounted. While one had little hope of saving society, one might at least have a part in saving men's souls.

Moreover, the value of anti-social activism served as an insulating mechanism for cultural fundamentalism itself. Without social inactivity, the beliefs, values and cultural orientation toward the world would have had great difficulty remaining plausible. The value of anti-social activism supported and protected the subculture. It limited the exposure of fundamentalists to opposing forces and competing worldviews, thereby enhancing the fundamentalist cultural orientation and belief system. According to Peter Berger, complex legitimations arise in situations where the belief system and the plausibility structure are threatened in one way or another. As part of cultural fundamentalism, social inaction helped to insulate the fundamentalist worldview against opposing worldviews.

---

[20]Chafer, *Systematic Theology*, 7:177.

Sociopolitical inactivity was taken for granted among fundamentalists and was preached from their pulpits as a defense against worldliness and as an impetus to keep people's minds on the primary commission of spreading the Gospel. In time the anti-social action value became a well understood, informal policy to guide and police younger generations.

Chapter Two

> *Question:* Do your people want to hear a personal, comforting message from the pulpit or are they interested in hearing about working for a better society?
>
> *Dixon:* My people want the comforting message. They would rather hear the pastor than the prophet.

The Moral Majority

In the fifty years that followed the Scopes Trial fundamentalists viewed societal change as possible only indirectly through the regenerated individual. Man's work was to bring men to Christ, not to deal with social evils. But in the late seventies some of the more vocal fundamentalists such as Jerry Falwell, Timothy LaHaye, Greg Dixon and others, began to act as though only aggressive political action could "save" society. Society's survival depended upon the triumph of the morally righteous—the conservative Christians—or perhaps even the Moral Majority. In 1965 Falwell proclaimed:

> Believing the Bible as I do, I would find it impossible to stop preaching the pure saving gospel of Jesus Christ, and begin doing anything else—including fighting communism, or participating in civil rights reforms....Preachers are not called to be politicians but to be soul winners....Nowhere are we commissioned to reform *the externals*. The gospel does not clean up the outside but rather regenerates the inside(quoted in Hadden and Swann, 1981:60).

Contrast this with the following statement made by Falwell in 1976:

> The idea that religion and politics don't mix was invented by the Devil to keep Christians from running their own country. If [there is] any place in the world we need Christianity, it's in Washington. And that's why preachers long since need to get over that intimidation forced upon us by liberals that if we mention anything about politics, we are degrading our ministry.(Goodman and Price, 1981:91).

It should be pointed out that not all fundamentalists support the Moral Majority's foray into political activism. Many fundamentalists feel that Falwell is dead wrong to abandon the traditional policy of separationism. Neuhaus maintains that there may be more fundamentalists who believe that Falwell was closer to the truth in 1965 when he proclaimed that he would never do anything other than preach the Gospel, than he was in 1980 when he changed his mind (1984:40). Sociologist Robert Bellah agrees with Falwell that America is "broken" and in need of "fixing," though he disagrees with Falwell as to what must be done to repair it (Bellah, 1975:1; cf. Hadden, 1985:26).

The validity and necessity of the social-separatist stance that cultural fundamentalism had supported for fifty years seemed to be diminished. What in particular contributed to the break in the fundamentalist self-imposed ban on sociopolitical action? Many factors contributed to this change in behavior, including a rise in social location since World War II (see Chapter 4 and Appendix A), strong, charismatic leadership (charismatic in Weber's sense, not in the Pentecostal sense), a network of dedicated persons with organizational talents, financial resources, and the fear that Christian civilization was threatened with extinction. Cultural fundamentalists, as opposed to cultural modernists, became ripe for political mobilization in the mid- to the latter part of the 1970's. It is this particular time period in which the volatile social issues concerning abortion, marijuana legalization, the Equal Rights Amendment and gay rights appeared on the political agenda (McIntire, 1979).

Though engagement in political activism has not been valued in the past, today it becomes apparently permissible for born-again fundamentalists to fight government policies which are perceived as immoral or against traditional values. It is not only the Moral Majority and other far right zealots who are fed up with what they see as an invasion by government and the courts into their private lives, but "by and large, the American people are indeed fed up with what they see as an invasion by government and the courts into their private lives. They are worried about the moral standards of the television programs seen by their children" (Stacks, 1981). If fundamentalist Christians are motivated to political action today, they are apparently responding to emotional and spiritual concerns rather than for the sake of material self-advantage. This idea is supportive of Hofstadter's position that status politics largely revolves around perceived threats or grievances in given value areas (cf. Patel et al., p.15). But it is also consistent with Fenn (1972:31) where he maintains that a dimension of religiosity may be an "activity which is an end in itself, and which is precisely what it appears to be, i.e., a search for 'truth or transcendent'" or ethical behavior.

Critics of the Moral Majority are tempted to view them as fanatics. Take the abortion issue, for example. It is an issue in which there is little room to compromise, to take a middle position. Legislatures, courts, and contending groups are caught in a bind, and issues such as this tend to become polarized. If one cannot imagine any middle ground, one might attempt to make opponents look like extremists. This contributes to making all persons feel as though they are occupying the reasonable, moderate position, in comparison with their opponents (cf. Yinger and Cutler, 1982:304).

Though Falwell is still preaching premillennialist theology, he now believes that "if Americans will face the truth, our nation can be turned around and can be saved from the evils and the destruction that have fallen upon every nation that has turned its back on God" (Falwell, 1980:18). Hadden believes that the "dominion covenant" is tugging at Falwell's soul. "If the individual is compelled to choose between good and evil, and if God has a plan for America, then it falls to each individual to join in the struggle" (Hadden, 1985:26). This is how Greg Dixon understands his own Moral Majority involvement in social activism. In a recent interview I asked the following:

> According to fundamentalist doctrine and world view, the world must get worse and worse before the end of time, when the Anti-Christ comes to rule on earth. This is considered to be one reason why born-again Christians have hesitated to become involved in social action. The world is doomed anyway. How is social action to be rationalized in light of this? Are we just postponing judgment?

Dixon responded:

> It is our responsibility to do right no matter what happens. The Lord will come anyway whether or not we work. For instance, if I were a member of the Sanhedrin during the time of Christ's crucifixion, I would not have voted for Christ to go to the cross just because this would hasten His plan. I would necessarily have voted

against it—knowing all the while that His plan would be done. Judas cannot say in the Day of Judgment that he helped Christ to the cross and thus to fulfill His plan. No, he is guilty no matter what. As Matthew says, "Offenses must come...." We do not hasten the Evil One just because it is in God's plan. The world will get worse anyway—but that doesn't mean I have to help it get worse.

The Bicentennial in 1976 may have had something to do with conservative Christian sentiment looking back to a romantic past (Noll, Hatch and Marsden, 1984).

This chapter presents the theoretical background and hypotheses for exploring how a fixed and well-understood plausibility structure known throughout most of the twentieth century for its support of an anti-secular, anti-social and antipolitical action orientation could seemingly yield behaviors contrary to the values of that worldview—values that could possibly spell out the rise of a new worldview and plausibility structure.

The Origins of the Moral Majority

When Jerry Falwell entered the national political scene in 1979, few political analysts were prepared to take him seriously. "Contemporary political analysts had come to see fundamentalism through the eyes of secularization theorists—as intermittent residual noise from an archaic religious form" (Hadden, 1985:18).

The Moral Majority was founded in June, 1979 by a group of pastors from very large Baptist churches around the country with memberships ranging in the thousands: Jerry Falwell (Thomas Road Baptist Church), James Kennedy (Fort Lauderdale Baptist Church), Charles Stanley (First Baptist Church of Atlanta), Tim LaHaye (Scott Memorial Baptist Church of San Diego), and Greg Dixon (Indianapolis Baptist Temple). Their common concern was to formulate a "nonpartisan political organization to promote morality in public life and to combat legislation that favored the legalization of immorality" (Falwell, 1981:188). Jerry Falwell is responsible for numerous operations: Thomas Road Baptist Church, Old Time Gospel Hour Radio Program, the Moral Majority,[1] Liberty University and the

---

[1]The Moral Majority is the largest and most prominent social movement organization in the New Christian Right (cf. Cable). It is, in fact, four separate organizations. Moral Majority, Inc., is a tax-exempt, but not tax deductible, lobbying arm organized to influence legislation at the

Liberty Foundation.[2] It is the Moral Majority that we focus on in this book. This is the "non-religious political" organization with which he hopes to turn American social practices around. Though Falwell maintains that the Moral Majority is separate from his "ministry," there seems to be no question that his multiple roles feed upon one another (cf. Hadden, 1985:21). Falwell has resigned as President of the Moral Majority, but has retained his position as Chairman of the Board.

Within two years of its inception the Moral Majority had chapters in all fifty states (Liebman, 1983),[3] numerous local affiliates, and an active Washington office which spent more than six million dollars in the fiscal year ending in August, 1981. Most of this money went to the Moral Majority's media campaign. Falwell must raise $100 million a year to keep the operation going. The Moral Majority report has an estimated readership at more than three million people (500,000 subscribers). More than 392 radio stations weekly broadcast the Old Time Gospel Hour and daily broadcast the Moral Majority Commentary. A bank of 62 telephone operators takes incoming pledges after the Old Time Gospel Hour program. A recent report indicates that Falwell has had to cut off its toll free line to save $7.2 million. This may spell out financial difficulties. Moral Majority claims to have over six and one half million members. However, outsiders figure membership to be much smaller. He has 110,000 pastors in the nation to draw on for support. Falwell has established 261 clinics around the country to assist pregnant women in having their babies and placing them for adoption, an outstanding feat in anybody's book.

In the minds of many people the Moral Majority has become the byword for the entire New Christian Right. Jerry Falwell personifies the movement for millions of Americans and this is probably due to the Old Time Gospel Hour,

---

national, state, and local levels. The Moral Majority Foundation is tax deductible. It was organized to educate ministers and lay people on crucial issues and to conduct voter registration drives. The Moral Majority Legal Defense Fund was organized to combat the American Civil Liberties Union and other "humanistic forces" through the courts. The Moral Majority Political Action Committee was set up to support political campaigns by morally conservative candidates (Shriver, 1981).

[2]He recently set up the Liberty Foundation which is the umbrella organization for the Moral Majority and includes organizational machinery to allow global participation in current foreign affairs.

[3]This has been questioned by Jeffrey K. Hadden and Charles E. Swann (1981).

Falwell's weekly religious program, and the prime time Jerry Falwell Specials that are occasionally broadcast, especially during election time.

The purposes of the Moral Majority include the following:

1) to educate voters on moral issues through newspapers, radio, television, seminars, ads, etc.,

2) to encourage voter registration and voter communication with representatives,

3) to inform voters of their representatives' voting records, and

4) to lobby in Congress to defeat legislation that would erode the traditional family and moral values.

Yinger and Cutler have developed an appropriate definition of the Moral Majority:

> ...a group with a highly organized center, surrounded by a sympathetic but relatively inactive ring. Those in the whole circle are dedicated to a set of moral and religious standards that they see threatened by "humanistic" forces in society—that is, by secularism, modernism, urbanism. They are opposed to the Equal Right Amendment, to the increased tolerance of homosexuality, the growing permissiveness regarding premarital sex, the greater acceptance of divorce, and to abortion, whether or not financed by government funds (Yinger and Cutler, 1982:291).

They react vociferously to government actions that get in the way of praying in schools, owning handguns, hiring whom they want, and living where they please...they feel assaulted by liberal government in a way that liberals do not feel assaulted by conservative government (Neuhaus, 1984:32).

One social issue that the Moral Majority will not become involved with apparently is the problem of poverty. To this Falwell has this response:

> We could never bring the issue of the poor into Moral Majority because the argument would be, who is going to decide what we teach those people? Mormons? Catholics? No, we won't get into that. As private persons and ministers, we make a commitment if we feel convicted. But for Moral Majority, no! If we go in there, create jobs, raise funds, and get involved with the local pastors, the problem is, which pastors? If we say the Mormon pastors, the fundamentalists are gone. If we say the Catholic pastors, the Jews

are gone, and so forth. We just have to stay away from helping the poor (*Christianity Today*, September 4, 1981, p. 27).

However, in the numerous homes for unwed pregnant women, the Moral Majority is helping "the poor." Falwell's initial refusal to use the Moral Majority to help the poor may be due to the fact that this action doesn't push his political agenda. Neither does it enhance the power of himself or the Moral Majority. Also, Falwell, along with many fundamentalists, believes that God gives financial rewards to the righteous. "Material wealth is God's way of blessing people who put him first" (quoted in Mayer, et al.: 35). Falwell tends to endorse policies that add property accumulation to big business, including labor discipline, lower taxes, anti-communism, heavy punishments for crimes against property and the free enterprise system in general. Falwell finds support for the free enterprise system in the book of Proverbs (Koenig and Boyce, 1983:4-5).

Falwell speaks of "fighting a holy war" to obtain his objectives. In international affairs the Moral Majority favors a peace through strength approach that endorses massive military buildup by the United States. They believe that an active public campaign to convert and persuade others is essential—a campaign designed not only to influence private actions and beliefs, but public policy as well (Yinger & Cutler, 1982:291). They believe an excessive emphasis on egalitarianism, affirmative action, school busing, and the welfare state is weakening the moral fiber of the nation.

Liberalism vs. Conservatism

Since I will be using terms such as "conservatism" and "liberalism" throughout the course of this work, it is important that we define our terms. Clinton Rossiter (1966) sets forth the definitions nicely.

Liberalism, Rossiter says, is the "stickiest word in the political dictionary." It is the "attitude of those who are reasonably satisfied with their way of life yet believe they can improve upon it substantially without betraying its ideals or wrecking its institutions" (1966:12). The liberal person attempts to take a balanced view of social processes, but when it comes to a showdown over some thoughtful plan to improve the lot of man, he will choose change over stability, experiment over continuity, the future over the past....He is optimistic rather than pessimistic about the possibilities of reform" (1966:12).

Conservatism "defends the social order against change and reform. The conservative knows that change is the rule of life among men and societies, but he insists that it be sure-footed and respectful of the past. He is pessimistic...about the possibilities of reform, and his natural preferences are for stability over change, continuity over experiment, the past over the future" (1966:12-13). The conservative has no illusions regarding the goodness of man, or his rationality.

While we can be sure that there is no visible line separating conservatism from liberalism, "in genuine liberals there is a sober strain of conservatism, in genuine conservatives a piquant strain of liberalism; all men, even extreme radicals, can act conservatively when their own interests are under attack" (1966:13).

As reactionaries, the New Right longs for the past and feels that a retreat back into it is worth the attempt. The true reactionary, Rossiter declares, is not conservative, but believes there was a time past when man were better off than they are in the present. "He is willing to erase some laws, enact others, even amend his nation's constitution—acting 'radically'—so that the social processes are rolled back to the time at which his countrymen first went foolishly astray" (1966:14). Here, then, separates Falwell from the older conservativetype.

The "Right" refers to those parties and movements that are skeptical of popular government, oppose the bright plans of the do-gooders, and draw support from men who have a stake in the established order. The "Left" refers to those parties and movements that demand wider participation in government, push actively for reform and may draw support from the disinherited, dislocated and disgruntled. Generally, the Right is conservative or reactionary, the Leftliberal or radical (Rossiter, p. 15). Fundamentalists who have joined the New Right as reactionaries would normally be considered "disinherited, dislocated, and disgruntled," however. It appears that it is their religious roots which have kept them from straying towards the Left.

Relation of the New Right to the Old Right

George Nash (1979:xvi) contends that "In 1945 no articulate, coordinated, self-consciously conservative intellectual force existed in the United States." The conservative movement that subsequently emerged was the intellectual component of the delayed right-wing Republican reaction to the New Deal, which surfaced in the early fifties and found political expression in McCarthyism (Himmelstein, 1983:18).

Nash interprets American conservatism to have developed as a synthesis of three intellectual tendencies: a libertarianism "apprehensive about the threat of the state to private enterprise and individualism," a traditionalism "appalled by the erosion of values and the emergence of a secular, rootless, mass society," and a militant anti-communism rooted in the "profound conviction that the West was engaged in a titanic struggle with an implacable adversary—communism—which sought nothing less than the conquest of the world" (xvi, 131).

Conservatism was not consolidated into a distinct intellectual world until the fifties and early sixties. In the next twenty years, within conservatism developed an "expanding cadre of intellectuals and a growing network of journals, research institutes and political organizations" (Himmelstein, p.20).

The New Right has its historical roots in American conservatism. The Moral Majority, a major component of the New Right, shares with conservatism a basic distrust of human nature and shares the conservative reaction to the romantic and liberal dogmas of human goodness and self-sufficiency (Niebuhr, 1932:526). Old Conservatism and the New Right both agree that during the sixties liberalism had gotten out of hand on college campuses, for example. In 1971, *National Review* published the results of a poll of undergraduates at twelve American campuses in 1969-70:

> Three-fifths [of the respondents] call themselves political liberals, fully 17% are self-proclaimed radicals...almost half favor the socialization of all basic industries; seven out of ten want their country unilaterally to suspend atomic weapons development. 40% say American society is "sick"; just over half believe that organized religion is harmful or worse. Given the alternatives of war or surrender in a confrontation with the Soviet Union, 54% would have the United States surrender (reported in Nash, 1979:304).

It wasn't just fundamentalist faith or conservative faith but it seemed that the American faith in the wisdom of higher education was tottering. Drugs, radicalism, changes in sexual standards, and estrangement from home all contributed to the disappointment in the educational system. "Where culture, civility, and learning were supposed to prevail, many Americans saw barbarism." William F. Buckley, Jr. was quoted as saying that he would rather be governed by the first 2,000 names in the Boston telephone book than by the entire Harvard faculty" (quoted in Nash, 1979:304).

The media was also seen to hold liberal positions on issues. It seemed to conservatives that the white middle class was continually portrayed by the media to be racist, authoritarian and banal, while the militant Left was seen as "harmless, friendly, idealistic, young, 'restless,' and trustworthy."

Conservatives came to the view that America itself was not "sick"; but liberalism was. It was the ruling elite; liberal universities, the media, some of the churches were sources of the profound malaise affecting the nation (Nash, 1979:306).

Though there have been occasional conflicts between the New Right and older conservative groups, these appear to be largely over tactics and turf, not ideology and goals. The New Right differs from the Old Right largely on matters of organizational strategy, not ideology (though there is evidence that the religious emphasis of the New Right bothers many in the Old Right. This is reflected in the mainstream Republican Party's rejection of Pat Robertson as candidate for the Presidency.) In respect to ideology, the New Right (of which the Moral Majority is the largest organization) is not really "new" at all. But in respect to organizational ability, tactics, and the religious orientation of the people involved, (i.e., fundamentalism), it is a relatively "new" phenomenon (cf. Himmelstein, p. 21).

It should be made clear that a small portion of what Yinger and Cutler call the "evangelical-fundamentalist revival" is not conservative in social outlook. This view is reflected in the *Sojourners* periodical that shares more of a leftist outlook. Political views represented here contrast sharply with those of the Moral Majority.

Another portion adheres to the traditional belief that religion and politics should not be mixed, and others feel that politics should be eschewed altogether—

as Falwell once believed. The latter feel that Falwell is betraying the Gospel by his commitment to social and political activism. It is this group who have not yet abandoned the logical implications of premillennial-dispensationalism. It is Falwell's shift from fundamentalist separatism to tangling in politics that has led Jeffrey Hadden (1985:19) to postulate a shift in doctrine from premillennial-dispensationalism to a post-millennial worldview. "Restoration of post-millennialism can provide the social movement with the conceptual or theoretical rationale for resuming the historic quest for dominion" (Hadden, 1985:19). While I think Hadden doesn't take fundamentalists' dedication to premillennial-dispensationalism seriously enough, his assessment does nicely point out the problem with social action involvement by premillennial-dispensationalists.

Pro-Social Action Stance of Moral Majority

Though they won the Scopes Trial, fundamentalism had been disgraced and was thought to be dying out as a social movement. Falwell himself states that the fundamentalist movement "was brought to an abrupt halt in 1925 at the Scopes Trial" (Falwell, 1981:90). As a result of its failure, it retreated and took a separatist stance on social and political issues. It was the results of the war with liberalism that produced the separatist sentiment (Weber, 1982:102).

> In our reaction against the social gospel, we have ignored the social implications of the gospel in conservative Christianity. In the past five years we became aware of that, and we acknowledged our wrong attitude. We must now make it a priority in the 80's (*Christianity Today*, 9-4-81, p. 26).

Both Falwell and Dixon say that they have no desire to Christianize the nation. Members of the Moral Majority just want their chance, like everybody else, to have their say. Falwell says he believes in a religious and cultural pluralism and has no intention of walking on anyone's First Amendment rights (Hadden and Swann, 1981:15). When I asked one Moral Majority leader what hopes the Moral Majority actually had in achieving a Christian society, he replied that it was "not our aim to achieve a Christian society but merely to insure that our rights to preach the Gospel and maintain our liberties are safe." This statement reveals the threatened status two major Moral Majority leaders have.

It seems that the Scopes Trial marks the time when fundamentalism as a movement became marked for its withdrawal or separatist stance on social action and political involvement. Historically, when fundamentalists lost an argument to modernists or liberals, they often responded by removing themselves one step further from social and political involvement. In reaction to the fundamentalist-modernist controversy, fundamentalism became more oriented toward evangelism, involving itself more in biblical conferences, missions and church building. It turned its focus from fighting modernism to building churches, schools, and fundamentalist colleges.

> This withdrawal and separatist position became a leading characteristic of the fundamentalist movement and caused fundamentalism to be blasted by religious and secular liberals for its anti-social and anti-political concerns and involvement. Rather than fighting, fundamentalists withdrew from the liberal seminaries, churches and schools and established their own (Falwell, 1981:91).

Quebedeaux maintains that fundamentalism's separatist stance applies basically to personal ethics—"as there is no social ethic" (Quebedeaux, 1978:22). To be "separate" in the realm of personal ethics usually means that fundamentalists abstain from the use of alcoholic beverages, tobacco and illegal drugs. Dancing and the secular theatre are also out of bounds as is pre- or extramarital sex. When Quebedeaux states that "there is no social ethic," he means that fundamentalists do not normally engage in purely secular activities—and this includes the public arena of politics. "Ethics" has nothing to do with how committed Christians treat others collectively (Quebedeaux, 1978:22). The fundamentalist understanding of social ethics does not include social programs, or public treatment of groups of people. The fundamentalist ethic is limited to person-to-person interaction. This is one reason fundamentalists have difficulty articulating political positions to non-fundamentalists.

Within the confines of the fundamentalist cultural orientation these separatist "convictions" have been based on a fundamentalist interpretation of Scripture. Though some fundamentalists are separatist and others are "open," (see Chapter One), practically all fundamentalists since the twenties have refrained from not only secular social activities, but also the social aspects of the ministry. The responsibility for Christian social work was abdicated in favor of stressing what was considered to be a purely spiritual ministry—evangelism, or saving people's souls. The reason for the abdication of this social responsibility is partly due to the fear that fundamentalists themselves may be swayed from the narrow truth of the Gospel. They had seen it happen within the mainline churches and felt it was their responsibility to guard strictly the sacred truths of Christendom as nobody else seemed to be doing it. Being weak in social and political involvement, fundamentalists have tended to proclaim their message in a strongly confrontational style. Falwell states:

> In a sincere attempt to maintain strict fundamentalism, (fundamentalists) have overtly labelled, categorized and castigated almost everybody. This has caused fundamentalists to attack each other as well (Falwell, 1981:170).

It is no secret that fellow fundamentalists are often their own worst enemies in attacking and criticizing what each other is trying to do or not to do in the name of Christ. During the fifty year "gap" in which fundamentalists as a whole deliberately kept aloof from American politics and social action involvement (causing the fundamentalist-evangelical rift in the 1940's), there had been only an occasional voice striking out against perceived threats to fundamentalist values— such as a Carl McIntire striking out at the liberal establishment or a Billy James Hargis stirring up anti-communist fears. But these figures never attracted more than a small fringe of fundamentalists and failed to establish active political organizations. It was due to their theological views and social status that fundamentalists had not been mobilized politically and had not shown much interest in politics (cf. Wuthnow, 1983:174). Involvement in the sociopolitical arena was considered to be "an evil of the flesh" at worst and an exercise in futility at best. Only by changing man's nature through repentance and salvationcould true societal change be expected.

Evangelical and fundamentalist domains of social concern are different. The older evangelical conservatism is considered to be dignified, scholarly, and middle class. They may be associated with the "Chicago call" (of 1773 to social action). A newer wing of evangelicals that would differ from the older element would be those associated with *Sojourners* magazine, and the Evangelicals for Social Action organization. This contingency is oriented more toward the Left, politically speaking. Fundamentalists are the newcomers to the social action scene and they are represented by a more demonstrative, aggressive, working-class group of hitherto anti-social action fundamentalists. These groups do not collaborate. Fundamentalists share a history of disengagement from the public order, a strong commitment to biblical authority, and a fervent determination to realize God's will on earth. The New Christian Right consists of this fundamentalist wing of social activists, not the evangelical Left or evangelical Right (cf. Hill and Owen, 1982:30).

It wasn't until the latter seventies that fundamentalist sects became involved in politics. What propelled the fundamentalists into social action? Against the background of pro-abortion legislation, movements for gay and women's rights, and a perception that President Carter had let "born-again" Christians down in his support for gay rights, the sharp line between the "kingdom of God" and the "kingdom of Caesar" began to blur for some fundamentalists. Sensing that the nation was in a moral crisis, many fundamentalists who were hitherto politically inactive now shifted their attention to the sphere of public life (Liebman: 227). The issue in the twenties was liberalism as a threat to conservative Christianity in terms of Darwin's theory, German Higher Criticism and the social gospel movement; in the seventies it appeared to be the same threat that was bothering many fundamentalist Christians—humanism, secularism, and moral decay in terms of abortion rights, homosexual rights, and attacks on Christian educational institutions (Falwell, 1980:144).

> Back in the sixties I was criticizing pastors who were taking time out of their pulpit to involve themselves in the Civil Rights Movement or any other political venture. I said you're wasting your time from what you're called to do. Now I find myself doing the same thing and for the same reasons they did. Things began to happen. The invasion of humanism into the public school system began to alarm us back in the sixties. Then the Roe vs. Wade Supreme Court decision of 1973 and abortion on demand shook me up. Then adding to that gradual regulation of various things it became very apparent the federal government was going in the wrong direction and if allowed would be harassing non-public schools, of which I have one of 16,000 right now. So step by step we became convinced we must get involved if we're going to continue what

we're doing inside the church building (quoted in Petersen and Board, 1980:18-19).

Actually, Falwell was not doing "the same thing" nor "for the same reasons" as those involved in the Civil Rights Movement. Whites involved in the Civil Rights Movement tended to belong to the more liberal element of Protestantism—not fundamentalism. But Falwell was shaken up. The government was increasingly becoming a threat to Christian private schools; humanism has always been a threat to fundamentalism (this time embodied in sex education, teaching evolution, and attacks on voluntary prayer in public schools), and the abortion ruling bothered Falwell as it did other conservative Christians.

Modern fundamentalists believe that contemporary public schools, for example, do not even remotely resemble schools of their childhood. Some Christian school activists view contemporary education as hostile to "American" values as evidenced in the recent Tennessee and Alabama textbook trials. In his well-publicized interview in *Penthouse* magazine, co-founder of the Moral Majority, Greg Dixon, asserted that the public school system basically "is atheistic, politically it is socialistic and philosophically it is relativistic."

The idea that schools were once heavily Protestant, but now are more humanistic, if not atheistic, pervades the ideology of the Moral Majority. It is often claimed that the real motivation for founding religious schools (fundamentalist in particular) is to discriminate racially against minorities. More is at stake here than racism. In the minds of many fundamentalists, public schools are seen as Godless, atheistic, immoral and as a tool for the state to control their children.

Since public schools teach Darwin's evolutionary scheme,

Evolution is the root of atheism, of communism, Naziism, behaviorism, racism, economic imperialism, militarism, libertinism, anarchism, and all manner of anti-Christian systems of belief and practice. A solid faith in a personal, sovereign Creator, on the other hand, leads to a strong sense of responsibility before God... (Morris, 1972:56).

Fundamentalists perceive the spread of secular humanism rules out consideration of God. Secular humanism is limited in that it views the world only in material terms. It abandons theistic foundations for traditional freedoms, and treats religion as an illusion.

However, secular humanism, according to Noll, Hatch and Marsden (1984), has always been a part of America's heritage. Even fundamentalism has a dose of humanism inherent in it, for example, the belief in self-help, the ability of a free people to solve their own problems and "rugged individualism." What particularly is upsetting to fundamentalists is what Noll, et al. would call "relativistic secularism" as a modern reality that is indeed powerful, widespread, and antagonistic to Christian faith" (p. 128).

In the late seventies vocal fundamentalists began to engage in confrontational social actions to protect family life and "standards of decency." Their outrage culminated in the creation of hundreds of organizations whose purpose was to stem the tide of pornography, to challenge gay rights legislation or to keep sex education out of the public schools. Some groups defended Christian schools from the threats of losing their tax exempt status; others fought the imposition of state certification requirements for private school teachers. Protecting religious broadcasting empires from the actions of the Federal Communications Commission and defending church organizations under the scrutiny of the Securities and Exchange Commission were other areas of involvement. Massive letter writing campaigns were organized, expensive legal talent was secured and hearing rooms were packed with fervent supporters of their causes (Liebman: 228).

Though most of these groups had dissolved by the end of the decade and early eighties, the Moral Majority, Christian Voice, and the Religious Roundtable have lasted and have issued a strong call for fundamentalists to take a stand in American political life. They were joined by the American Coalition for Traditional Values (Tim LaHaye), Conservative Caucus (Howard Phillips), National Christian Action Coalition (Robert Billings), and other New Right groups. They saw it as their God-given duty to make their voices heard. They were the "salt of the earth" and the conscience of the nation. If America fell from greatness, it would partly be due to their silence.

Through meetings, mailings, media campaigns, and massive voter registration drives, vocal fundamentalist leaders sought to mobilize their constituents, evangelicals and other morally conservative Americans into a strong political bloc. It was their duty to engage in the political process as a means of bringing America back to God. Like the liberals of the fifties and sixties they believed that morality could be legislated. Therefore it was important to get the right people elected to Congress (Hadden and Swann: 134). Of all the New Right groups, the Moral Majority was the most successful in terms of having the greatest impact in society. This is most likely due to its connection to the network of Independent Baptist churches (Liebman, 1983). Seventy-five percent of the respondents to my survey were Independent Baptist while 99% were fundamentalist (see Appendix C).

Relation of the Moral Majority to Cultural Fundamentalism

Since the mid-twenties fundamentalism has supported evangelism and orthodox beliefs as their main thrust. The social aspects of the ministry were left to liberal Protestants to worry about and politics were generally eschewed except for the private role of voting. Voting usually was considered to be unrelated to religious activities.

These patterns of behavior and expectation were understood and accepted unquestioningly by fundamentalists. The fact that today political action by Falwell and other fundamentalists is being attacked by fellow-fundamentalists who share the same religious beliefs (cf. Guth, 1983), demonstrates how well understood and taken-for-granted this informal policy of sociopolitical separatism has been.

It is clear that Moral Majority leaders have no intention of leaving behind their fundamentalist religious beliefs, however. Rather than moving to a post-millennial stance as Hadden (1985) suggests, my sample demonstrates Guth's (1983) contention that Moral Majoritarian members are "monotonously orthodox" in theological orientation. They are as ready as their fundamentalist predecessors of the twenties to fight humanism, secularism and human decay. It is as if this current vocal element in the Moral Majority has backed up fifty years to fight the same enemy—only this time with more knowledge, expertise and resources at their disposal.

Moral Majoritarians perhaps have been able to remain true to fundamentalist doctrinal beliefs, but they have not been able to remain faithful to the social implications, values, and expected patterns of behavior of premillennial-dispensationalism. Jerry Falwell quotes Proverbs 14: "Living God's principles promotes a nation to greatness; violating God's principles brings a nation to shame." Herein lies one of his rationales for promoting social activism among his fundamentalist contingency. Because social activism is not the expected outcome from those who espouse the doctrinal tenets of premillennial-dispensationalism, one might expect a measure of cognitive dissonance to result by fundamentalists who engage in social activism. This was a major hypotheses in this study (see Chapter Three).

Chapter Three

Research Method

Data

Data were obtained through the use of questionnaires (See Appendix D).

Mailing lists of the Moral Majority of Indiana dated January, 1983 served as the data source for this study. A scientific random sample was drawn from two of the lists, (1) donors (N = 1205) and (2) clergy including board of directors and county chairmen (N = 550). Three hundred ninety respondents consisting of 105 clergymen, 224 donors and 10 District Chairmen were sent questionnaires.[1] After two follow-up mailings, 46 clergymen and 116 donors returned usable questionnaires yielding a return rate of 48% (N = 162).

Returned questionnaires included two county chairmen, two district chairmen, and five members of the board of directors. All but one of the clergy and officials of the Moral Majority were male. But the donors consisted of both sexes. Males made up 69% of the respondents and 46% of non-respondents. Women made up 31% of respondents and 27% of non-respondents. Married couples (as printed on the mailing list) made up 24% of non-respondents and I was unable to determine the sex on 3 % of the non-respondents from the names on the mailing list.

Multiple regression analysis, correlation coefficients, cross-tabulations and percentages are used throughout the book to test various relationships among variables.

Regression equations are used to test for intergenerational mobility and its effects on one's adherence to the New Right versus the cultural fundamentalist

---

[1]Originally 414 questionnaires were mailed out but 390 remained after removing those who had changed residences.

plausibility structure. Regression equations are also used to test for susceptibility to leadership.

Pearson Correlation coefficients are used to test the relationship of plausibility structures to social action behavior, social action values, cognitive dissonance, and cognitive dissonance reducing mechanisms.

Percentages are used to get an overview of actual social action behaviors, attitudes about social action behaviors, rationales and legitimating mechanisms for use in conducting social action and in reducing cognitive dissonance due to social action behaviors. Numerous other questions throughout the text are illustrated with use of percentage rates of response.

Interviews with Greg Dixon and other Moral Majority leaders were also instrumental in providing me with specific information and giving me insight into the thinking of Moral Majority leaders.

Using data gathered from one chapter of the Moral Majority to make assessments about the national body of Moral Majority members is not without its problems. The major question is, can I generalize to the full population of Moral Majority members what my research reveals about the Indiana chapter? One would think that the colorful figure and personality of Rev. Greg Dixon has influenced the membership of the Moral Majority in Indiana. For example, while Jerry Falwell has claimed that Mormons, Jews and Catholics are also part of the Moral Majority, the sample from Indiana does not support this. While I believe that the attitudes and behaviors of the Indiana members on the issues are similar to the attitudes of members nationally, I did not sample the national body and did not test for this so I cannot conclusively demonstrate this. I will say that if a researcher could access the national membership, much could be learned about the Moral Majority membership nationally.

Measurement of Variables

The variables and scales used in testing hypotheses are presented below. See Appendix D for the entire questionnaire.

Measure I.   Strength of Ties to Fundamentalist Plausibility Structure

Items depicting ties to the Moral Majority plausibility structure involve things such as friends in the Moral Majority, hours given to Moral Majority activities in a month, length of time a Moral Majority member, and whether respondent does/has held office in the Moral Majority. The higher one scores here, the more tightly bonded to the Moral Majority plausibility structure. The following four items comprise the "strength of ties to the Moral Majority plausibility structure" scale. The weight of each item is determined by the response category.

How many of your closest friends are active in the Moral Majority?

About how many hours do you devote to the Moral Majority in an average month?

How long have you been a member of the Moral Majority?

Do you hold or have you recently held any office in your local Moral Majority?

The reliability of this scale is indicated by a Cronbach's Alpha of .47.

Measure II. Engagement in Social Action Behaviors

Here are specific social actions that a respondent might have engaged in:

Given money to support a political candidate.

Donated money to a political organization that was not related to religion.

Displayed an American flag at my home.

Taken part in a rally against an immoral activity in my community.

Written my congressman in support of a larger defense budget.

Written my congressman on a foreign policy issue.

Choices for the first two items were: (1) yes, (2) no. For the last four items choices were (1) I've never taken this action, (2) The first time I took this action was less than five years ago, (3) The first time I took this action was more than five years ago. If respondents had preferred these actions at all (in categories 2 or 3) they were given a point.

The reliability of this scale is indicated by a Cronbach's Alpha of .63.

Measure III.   Social Action Values

To test for *values* of social action we have chosen the following items:

Ministers have a responsibility to speak out as the moral conscience of the nation.

Ministers should stick to religion and not concern themselves with social, economic and political questions.

I am happy for my minister to participate actively in social causes.

I want my minister to feel free to give a sermon on any social or political issue he strongly supports.

The church should direct some of its activities toward changing the structure of American society.

Choices for these five items were: (1) Strongly Agree, (2) Agree, (3) Undecided, (4) Disagree, (5)Strongly Disagree.

These questions relate to the involvement of ministers and the church to social action issues. Because of the anti-social action values inherent in the fundamentalist worldview, this scale is especially helpful in revealing to what extent Moral Majority members have adopted pro-social action values.

The reliability of this scale is indicated by a Cronbach's Alpha of .73.

Measure IV.   Social Action Activities since the founding of the Moral Majority

We asked respondents which of the following behaviors they engaged in and at what time intervals:

Displayed an American flag at my home.

Taken part in a rally against an immoral activity in my community.

Written my congressman in support of a larger defense budget.

Written my congressman on a foreign policy issue.

Choices for these four items were: (1) I've never taken this action, (2) The first time I took this action was less than five years ago, (3) The first time I took this action was more than five years ago.

While these four items do not provide an exhaustive list of possible social actions Moral Majority members might engage in (see the social activism scale above for a wider range of possible social action activities), these items do offer a description and an estimation of social action activities which Moral Majority supporters might have been mobilized to engage in due to the influence of the Moral Majority. This is not a "scale" and is used for descriptive purposes only, not prediction (see Table 5.3).

Measure V. Attitudes on Social Action Behavior

The following items comprise an attitude scale relating to various kinds of social action behaviors people might engage in:

Take action such as either boycotting or getting up a petition.

Hold public speeches and rallies.

Stage mass demonstrations with large crowds of people.

March quietly and peacefully through town.

Choices for these four items include: (1) Yes, (2) No. This is not a scale to be used for prediction; it is used for descriptive purposes only.

Measure VI. Susceptibility to Leadership Scale

The following items comprise the susceptibility to leadership scale:

The leaders of the Moral Majority have the answers I want and I am grateful for those answers.

The Moral Majority's leaders help me clarify my values so that I can see that their decisions are right.

The Moral Majority's leaders motivate me to think things through and come out with the best answers whether or not I agree with them.

The Moral Majority's leaders give me the information I need to reach my own conclusions.

Choices for these four items were: (1) Strongly Agree, (2) Agree, (3) Undecided, (4) Disagree, (5) Strongly Disagree.

The reliability of the scale is indicated by a Cronbach's Alpha of .72.

Measure VII. Cognitive Dissonance

Cognitive dissonance is best measured in clinical settings where stress and uneasiness can be measured as it occurs. In questionnaire survey research, cognitive dissonance is difficult to test. But by asking the respondent about his or her uneasiness toward engaging in a certain action, we can access limited knowledge as to whether the respondent is experiencing or has experienced cognitive dissonance due to social activism.

A cognitive dissonance scale was devised from four questions. The first question asked the following:

> Sometimes it bothers me to be involved in social and political action activities.

If agreed with the statement, the respondent received one point. If the respondent disagreed with the statement, the follow-up question was asked:

> Can you remember a time when it did bother you to be engaged in social and political action activities?

If respondents answered in the affirmative to this follow-up question, they received one point.

The respondents scoring on this scale are those expected to have made use of cognitive dissonance reducing mechanisms to reduce the state of uneasiness experienced because of their social and political actions. If respondents replied in the negative to this follow-up question indicating that they presently do not, nor do they ever recall being bothered by their engagement in sociopolitical activities, either (1) this person has never experienced uneasiness due to engagement in social activism, or (2) they did experience dissonance, but have since repressed the dissonance or have rationalized it so that they themselves do not recall ever having been bothered by engagement in social or political issues. Though Festinger does not address the possibility of a subject's lack of awareness of his dissonance, researchers disagree on the issue as to whether minimal awareness is necessary if dissonance is to be a motivating force (Brehm and Cohen, 1962: McGuire, 1960; Feldman, 1966). It would seem that a person should recognize the particular inconsistency that is causing dissonance, as well as the dissonance itself.

The third question asked respondents the following:

Do you see any contradiction between social activism and evangelism?

Respondents responding in the affirmative received one point.

For those who reported seeing no contradiction between evangelism and social activism, the following question was asked:

Did you ever see any contradiction between social activism and evangelism?

A person could score from zero to two points on the cognitive dissonance scale. A score of zero would imply that the respondent had experienced no cognitive dissonance regarding social action issues; one point would mean he/she experienced "some" cognitive dissonance and a score of two points would imply that the respondent had experienced a good deal of cognitive dissonance. Those who report never having seen the contradiction between social activism and evangelism can either (1) be taken at face value, e.g., they truly have never seen a contradiction between social action and evangelism; or (2) they were unaware of any contradiction between social action and evangelism in the fundamentalist worldview; or (3) they have seen the contradiction between social action and evangelism but have repressed or rationalized this awareness away (see discussion above and Chapter Five).

Measure VIII. Cognitive Dissonance Reducing Mechanisms

Cognitive dissonance reducing mechanisms came from two sources in the questionnaire. (1) I asked those who presently or in the past saw a contradiction between social activism and evangelism how they resolved this contradiction (see question 102b in Appendix D). The answers to this open-ended question provided one source of cognitive dissonance reducing mechanisms used to resolve the inherent conflict respondents saw between social activism and evangelism. (2) For those who replied having been bothered by engagement in social action activities I provided three "reasons" why they might have been bothered (see questions 105b, 105c, 105d in Appendix D). They are:

> It is God's plan that the world must worsen until the Anti-Christ comes to rule on Earth.

> Christians should concentrate on spreading the gospel.

Choices for these items were: (1) Strongly Agree, (2) Agree, (3) Undecided, (4) Disagree, (5) Strongly Disagree.

The reliability of the scale is indicated by a Cronbach's Alpha of .57.

Measure IX. Socioeconomic Status

The socioeconomic status measure consists of a scale made up of income plus education plus occupation for laypersons. For clergy, socioeconomic status consisted of income plus education (occupational category was uniform).

Income. (See item 191 in Appendix D).

Education. (See item 193 in Appendix D).

Occupation. (See item 192 in Appendix D).

Occupations were collapsed into a sevenfold class schema devised by Goldthorpe (1980:39-42). Goldthorpe's model was taken from Goldthorpe and Hope (1974:131-143). This schema provides a relatively high degree of differentiation in terms of occupational function and employment status. The associated employment status is treated as part of the definition of an occupation.

Measure X. Intergenerational Change in Social Status

Intergenerational change in social status consists of three variables which are used to compare additive and interactive models determining the effects of change in social status on ties to plausibility structures. The additive model consists of respondents' educational level (destination effects) and fathers' educational level (origination effects) as predictors of ties to plausibility structures. The interactive model adds interaction effects to origination and destination effects for predicting ties to plausibility structures. The interaction variable represents the impact of social mobility per se, exclusive of origination and destination effects, and consists of respondent's education minus father's education.[2]

Theoretical Assumptions
Theoretical assumptions that underlay this work include the following:
1. Cultural fundamentalism has had a tradition of devaluing involvement in social activism since the Scopes Trial.
2. Fundamentalists in the Moral Majority are actively engaging in social activism.
3. Social activism creates a contradiction for those tied to premillenial-dispensationalism and should result in a state of cognitive dissonance.
4. This cognitive dissonance ought to motivate politically active fundamentalists to do one of three things: (a) stop the social activism, (b) employ cognitive dissonance reducing mechanisms while continuing the engagement in social activism, or (c) leave the cultural fundamentalist plausibility structure.

We cannot test option (a) in the fourth theoretical assumption using cross-sectional data. This test would logically require that fundamentalists not be Moral Majoritarians. We can, however, test options (b) and (c). These options will be focused on in chapters four and five.
See Appendix C for complete table of descriptive statistics for measures.

---

[2]The comparison of the additive and interactive models to test for the effect of social mobility per se is thoroughly outlined in David Knoke, "Intergenerational Occupational Mobility and the Political Party Preferences of American Man," in the *American Journal of Sociology* 78:6, pp. 1448-1468.

Chapter Four

Plausibility Structures

To live in an ordered world, people actively construct schemes with which they classify and order the reality around them. When contradicted or confused, "pollution behaviors" may be resorted to in order to deal with this "dirt" (Douglas, 1966:35-6). Peter Berger (1977) and Berger and Luckmann (1967:154-155) have coined the term "plausibility structure" to explain how it is that people can maintain a particular view of reality of the world in the face of opposing views of reality. Accordingly, any conception of the world may be analyzed in terms of its supporting plausibility structure because it is only as the individual remains within this structure that the conception of the world in question will remain plausible (Berger, 1984). Subjective reality especially is dependent on "plausibility structures." The strength of plausibility will range from absolute certainty to mere opinion and depends on the strength of the supporting structure. Each plausibility structure can be analyzed in terms of its constituent elements—the human beings that compose it, the conversational network utilized to maintain the view of reality, the therapeutic practices and rituals, and the legitimations that go with them. In this sense all people belong to one or more plausibility structures. For example, a young person originally accepts given notions about the world from his or her parents. The definitions of the child's situation are posited for the child as objective reality and accepted as such. The child thereby takes on the roles and attitudes of significant others and in the same process adopts their "world" as well (Berger and Luckmann, 1967). Individuals do not form, develop, or act on attitudes in a vacuum but rather in a network of social interactions. A worldview or interpretation of reality can only maintain its plausibility if it has adequate support.

Social location plays a crucial role in determining one's plausibility structure, but at the same time it is a part of that plausibility structure. Sociologists of knowledge teach that one's social position is a powerful determinant of the meanings that are ascribed to events. For example, "insiders" to a religious group may believe that the suffering of children is evidence of the visitation of God's wrath on the sins of their parents, while "outsiders" may interpret the same event as compelling evidence against the very existence of God (Snow and Machalek, 1982:24). Parents and significant others select aspects of their objective social world in accordance with their own location in the social structure. A particular social world is thus presented to the child through the social location filter, making social class a crucial determinant of the plausibility structure. Ideas will remain credible as long as significant others continue to affirm them.

As individuals increase their exposure to a variety of social networks or "conversational fabrics," they may find contradictions and complexities interfering with their conceptions of the universe. If this happens, they often will be confronted with organized practices or "therapies" from the plausibility structure in question which are designed to settle doubts and restrengthen conviction. Systematized explanations, justifications and theories, called "legitimations" or "legitimating mechanisms" are used to support or reestablish the conceptions in question. But because socialization and/or mobility is never total or finished, there is always the possibility for a given plausibility structure to lose its hold on an individual and for a person to move into other plausibility structures thus leaving the old behind. Unconventional belief systems are usually more fragile and are considered to owe their persistence primarily to the power of the plausibility structure to keep tenuous beliefs intact (cf. Snow and Machalek, 1982).

Berger maintains that the social infrastructure of a particular ideational complex, along with various concomitant maintenance procedures, practical, as well as theoretical, constitutes its plausibility structure. They set the conditions within which the ideas in question have a chance of remaining plausible. Within the plausibility structure the individual encounters others who confirm by their attitudes and assumptions that the particular ideational complex is to be taken for granted as reality. Authority figures and officially accredited reality-definers play key roles in maintaining the plausibility structure (Berger, 1977:173). Berger points out that the ongoing social and psychological dynamics underlying plausibility structures especially pertains to religious ideation because religion is a collective enterprise. By their very nature religious beliefs are incapable of being supported by sense experience and are all the more heavily dependent upon social support.

To the extent that plausibility structures "exist," everyone makes use of them. Though the term "plausibility structure" is usually used when writers speak of highly subjective or unconventional beliefs—usually considered to be more unstable—it has been noted by others (i.e., Snow and Machalek, 1982) that there may be little qualitative difference between the plausibility structures advanced in support of unconventional beliefs and those associated with conventional or dominant realities. The point is being made that the "differential viability of belief systems cannot be accounted for merely in terms of underlying plausibility structures for it treats as unique to some groups that which is, in fact, commonplace. It also deflects attention from other possible sources of validation, thereby precluding a fuller understanding of the appeal and credibility of unconventional beliefs" (Snow and Machalek, 1982:18).

So, what, then, are we speaking of in terms of a special "fundamentalist plausibility structure" for this historical group of people who were a source of embarrassment before leaving the mainline, more "sophisticated" denominations if everybody uses plausibility structures to keep their various worldviews intact? What we're speaking of here is the fact that fundamentalists, as a result of disgrace after the Scopes Trial, deliberately constructed a "sub-plausibility structure," as Meredith McGuire (1982) calls it, to insulate their views from further attack and shame. A liberal Methodist doesn't have to be on guard when walking down Main Street. He isn't necessarily made to feel inferior when he encounters prominent business people because they are likely to be in a similar plausibility structure, if not the same one. The probabilities are not the same for a fundamentalist, or for that matter a Moonie, scientologist or Mormon. These groups have had to take special trouble establishing sub-plausibility structures that will enable them to continue in their beliefs with minimal vulnerability. If their plausibilities are "fragile," they will be on special guard wherever they go for those who might wish to "corrupt" them or scoff at them. They have developed legitimating mechanisms and rationales to handle this kind of difficulty. It is likely that what Lofland (1966) found to be true of the Unification belief system is equally true of the fundamentalist belief system: they are both designed so that all experience, all counter-arguments, would only produce confirmation" (Lofland, 1966:195). Snow and Machalek observe that some unconventional belief systems are amazingly resilient and apparently invulnerable to disconfirmation. "...A thorough understanding of the beliefs themselves may reveal some features that enable them to persist in the face of contradictory evidence." Bainbridge and Stark (1980) have discovered this "incredible" fact in their study of scientologists. The scientologist, like the fundamentalist, the Jehovah's Witness, and other millennial enthusiasts, can maintain faith in unfulfilled claims by invoking the unfalsifiable belief that "ultimately all the promised benefits will be provided" (Bainbridge and Stark, 1980:134). In this sense, plausibility structures operate to enhance what is logically self-perpetuating (Snow and Machalek, 1982:22). "Unlike belief in science, many belief systems do not require consistent and confirmatory evidence. Beliefs may even withstand the pressure of disconfirming evidence not because of the effectiveness of dissonance-reducing strategies, but because disconfirming evidence may simply go unacknowledged" (Snow and Machalek, 1982:23). Snow and Machalek do not deny that plausibility structures are important in validating beliefs, they explain how characteristics of belief systems themselves contribute to their perpetuation. They also suggest that evidence discrepant with belief does not necessarily create cognitive dissonance as belief systems may feature validation logics that help insure their persistence.

Fundamentalist groups have often been treated as a lunatic fringe of society (cf. Neuhaus, 1982, Hadden & Swann, 1981) that wasn't respectable enough to be considered when making political decisions. Partly because they have valued politics to be "dirty business" and partly because the political process had discounted their importance, they have developed feelings of powerlessness and second-class citizenship (Hadden and Swann, 1981:134).

The plausibility structures of religious groups originating in the lower socioeconomic groups often involve multi-weekly meetings and intimate relationships among adherents. Frequent contact and intimate concern among fundamentalists serve to reinforce the belief system and cultural orientation, thereby establishing a firm plausibility structure. Men and women are often called "brother" and "sister", emphasizing the closeness of the members of the group. In keeping with the limited outside organizational and societal involvement of the lower socioeconomic groups, fundamentalists often have limited their social circle to the local church group which often has claimed a monopoly on members' time, money and energy.

> The fundamentalist mind is essentially Manichean; it looks upon the world as an arena for conflict between absolute good and absolute evil, and accordingly scorns compromises (who would compromise with Satan?) and can tolerate no ambiguities. It cannot find serious importance in what it believes to be trifling degrees of difference: liberals support measures that are for all practical purposes socialistic, and socialism is nothing more than a variant of communism, which, as everyone knows, is atheism...the cold war [is] a clash of faiths....The issues of the actual world are hence transformed into a spiritual Armageddon, an ultimate reality, in which any reference to day-to-day actualities has the character of an allegorical illustration...(Hofstadter, 1966:135).

As do most people, fundamentalists associate with others within their social infra-structure who confirm their beliefs and cultural orientation. The attitudes and assumptions of those within this social infrastructure, such as family members, friends, and pastors, support and confirm the accepted worldview of fundamentalism. Adhering to the traditional "televangelists" of the electronic church also confirms and supports this belief system as most contemporary televangelists are fundamentalists.

Berger notes that strongly integrated belief systems tend to produce firm objectivations and are capable of supporting worldviews and ideas with a firm status of objective reality within the consciousness of their adherents. An example of a fundamentalist firm objectivation is the notion that the world is evil and is ruled by Satan.

The fundamentalist worldview supports socially and subjectively convincing answers to just about every type of question that fundamentalists could ask. This has resulted in a strongly integrated, coherent belief system and cultural orientation.

As fundamentalists moved into the middle and upper middle classes following World War Two, their involvement with non-fundamentalist people and processes increased. The second and third generation fundamentalists tended to be college educated, employed in the professions and members of civic organizations and clubs. One might expect this increased exposure to have weakened their ties to cultural fundamentalism and to have caused some of those values and beliefs upheld by fundamentalism (such as social inactivism) to be called into question.

Eventually, certain fundamentalist leaders with fundamentalist backgrounds devised a new social agenda to fight social ills which were perceived to be getting worse and worse.

> Millions of Americans have for a long time felt put upon. Theirs is a powerful resentment against values they believe have been imposed upon them, an equally powerful sense of outrage at the suggestion that they are the ones who pose the threat of undemocratically imposing values upon others (Neuhaus, 1984:52).

Today, fundamentalists are capitalizing on a deep resentment. They believe that in the past they have been excluded and despised by the leadership elites in American life. Neuhaus says there is good reason for their feeling this way. "In fact they *have* been excluded and despised, excluded from respectable circles and made an object of ridicule in the 1920's" (Neuhaus, 1982:11).

Certain fundamentalist leaders provided the direction and the vehicle for a new policy of social activism. By capitalizing on the already constructed social reality and the salient beliefs necessarily inherent in fundamentalism, only slight modifications were needed to make a relatively "reasonable" argument for social activism in the late seventies. These leaders made social action a feasible and viable option for the army of fundamentalists with resources and courage to act. The numerous politico-religious televangelists of the electronic church and computerized mailing wizards such as Richard Viguerie (a Catholic, however) were also helpful in rousing the fundamentalist camp. Moreover, Jerry Falwell believes that on a majority of issues a majority of the American people agree with the Moral Majority. Increasingly, social critics are stating their agreement with Falwell's assessment (cf. Ostling, 1985; Neuhaus, 1982, 1984). Outside commentators agree with Falwell that there is a widespread feeling in America of spiritual bafflement and dissatisfaction. Rodney Stark thinks that the religious right "makes quite accurate assessments." Anti-religion and amorality have in fact been spreading in the public schools, Stark observes, and a majority of Americans are scandalized "by the apparent flouting of traditional values on television and in the press" (quoted in Ostling, 1985).

By engaging in cognitive manipulations (i.e., rationalizations, explanations and legitimating mechanisms), Moral Majority leaders have been able to provide the plausibility and even the necessity for a new policy of social activism. The new policy of social action could now be considered by socially active fundamentalists to be just as valid and necessary as the previously held policy of social inaction because their world outlook is so firm. The adoption of the new stance of sociopolitical activism is evidence that a new plausibility structure within fundamentalism is underway. Of course, there are many fundamentalists who do not see the necessity to engage in social action and this is probably because they have remained true to the behavioral implications of premillennial-dispensational theology and cultural fundamentalism. Fifteen years ago Falwell condemned Martin Luther King, Jr. and other ministers who were involved in the Civil Rights Movement. Falwell has since changed his mind on the social action issue, hundreds of fundamentalist pastors have also changed their minds, and it appears that thousands of fundamentalist laypersons are now in the process of changing their minds as well. It appears that these fundamentalists are now accepting the suppositions of the evangelicals that they disagreed with in the 1940's.

In sum, cultural fundamentalist values imply that fundamentalists should not become involved in social action concerns. Yet, fundamentalists making up the Moral Majority have adopted pro-social action values and behavior. This may mean that members of the Moral Majority are tied to a new plausibility structure supportive of social action. It is also possible that Moral Majoritarians have employed legitimating mechanisms that allow them to operate within the confines of cultural fundamentalism while not totally adhering to or believing in the behavioral patterns it promotes.

Legitimating Mechanisms for the Failure to Engage in Social Action

The fundamentalist cultural orientation is supported by complex legitimations which defend it when confronted with opposing views. For example, one legitimation given in the past for the failure of fundamentalists to engage in social action is that the world is lost or doomed. According to premillenial-dispensationalism which most fundamentalists have adopted, the world belongs to the kingdom of Satan and has been lost since the Fall of Man. Evangelism, therefore, has received legitimation whereas social action has been discounted. While one had little hope of saving society, one might at least have a part in "saving men's souls."

Moreover, the practice of social inactivity had a very practical use. It served as an insulating mechanism for cultural fundamentalism itself. With social activism, the beliefs, values and cultural orientation that fundamentalists have had toward the world would have had great difficulty remaining plausible. The value of social inaction supported and protected the subculture. Social inaction served to limit the exposure of fundamentalists to opposing forces and competing worldviews, thus enhancing the fundamentalist cultural orientation and belief system. Berger states that complex legitimations arise in situations where the belief system and the plausibility structure are threatened in one way or another (1967:47). As part of cultural fundamentalism, social inaction helped to insulate the fundamentalist worldview from opposing worldviews, or views that would threaten in some way their own outlook.

The social interaction patterns within fundamentalism became the basis of a subculture which supported certain beliefs, values and ways of thinking. Inherent in this subculture were patterns of limited association with those outside of their "world." These "disenfranchised" citizens socialized with each other and limited their meaningful interpersonal relationships to this limited social circle. The fundamentalist cultural complex involved firm objectivities and unwavering dogmatism which served to protect the fundamentalist worldview from opposing views. Anti-social action values were crucial as legitimating mechanisms to keep religious beliefs from weakening and supporting the solidarity of fundamentalism generally. Put another way, social inaction was taken for granted among fundamentalists and was preached from fundamentalist pulpits as a defense against "worldliness" and as an impetus to keep people's minds on the primary commission of "spreading the Gospel." In time this value of social inaction became a well-understood, informal policy to guide and police younger generations.

To understand how one acts in discordance with one's plausibility structure while remaining in it, or how people move from one plausibility structure to another, I pose the question: has the Moral Majority, made up of fundamentalist Christians, remained part of traditional fundamentalism, or have they moved out of the traditional fundamentalist plausibility structure, thus adopting or creating a new plausibility structure more supportive of sociopolitical action? Or have they simply rejoined their evangelical brothers and sisters in a plausibility structure that allows and legitimizes social activism? If Moral Majoritarians have remained within traditional fundamentalism, they would need to address the question of their sociopolitical involvement since the latter would be foreign to and not supported by the fundamentalist worldview as it exists and has been known for a half century after Scopes. In fact, socially active fundamentalists should be experiencing a degree of cognitive dissonance due to their acting contrary to expected fundamentalist behavioral patterns. Sociopolitical actions may be rationalized through the use of legitimating mechanisms. By appending necessary legitimating mechanisms to the fundamentalist worldview, socially active fundamentalists could "justify" their newfound interest and competence in social issues while remaining within the plausibility structure. Those who wish to take this tact of explaining the necessity of social activism by fundamentalists might make an argument such as the following:

> America was founded as a 'Christian nation.' But the nation turned from its Christian foundation and in recent decades has been taken over by secular humanism. The goal today is to become a Christian nation once again—by restoring America to its 'biblical base,' to the 'biblical principles of our founding fathers,' to a 'Christian consensus,' etc....The only alternative seems to be an all-out battle between the forces advocating a return to 'Christian America' and the ruling forces of 'secular humanism' so that America can become a Christian nation once again (Noll et al., p. 129).

However, if the Moral Majority has created a new plausibility structure, or joined one of the evangelical plausibility structures (as Jerry Nims and Jerry Falwell appear to have done by their statements that they are now "mainline evangelicals"), cognitive dissonance would not necessarily be a problem. The new plausibility structure would support political activism. Justifications, systematized explanations, or legitimations could be used to support the positive stance on social action. These would be incorporated into the new worldview as part of its "therapy" to keep members supportive of the new social action policy.

Meredith McGuire notes that when a religious group holds or develops a worldview which is not supported by the larger group to which it belongs, it must construct its own plausibility structure (McGuire, 1981:33). This may be what Falwell and his cohort have done through the establishment of the Moral Majority. They have "therapies," systematized explanations and justifications for their pro-social action stance, just as traditional fundamentalists have had their legitimations for withdrawing from social concerns. In this sense the Moral Majority may be the catalyst for creating a new kind of plausibility structure and worldview for the New Christian Right that supports sociopolitical activism. A difficulty with solving the social action problem by stating that the Moral Majority has simply become "evangelical" is that you still have the sociocultural and doctrinal emphases that distinguish them from the broader evangelical label. It will be interesting to see if Jerry Falwell and Jerry Nims, as Chairman of the Board and President of the Moral Majority, respectively, are able to sell the idea of an evangelical Moral Majority to both the constituents of the Moral Majority and the evangelical community.

Summary

These issues are crucial to our understanding of how political and social activities of Moral Majority members relate to the traditional subculture of fundamentalism. But more important for our sociological understanding of plausibility structures in general are the roles plausibility structures play in shaping the beliefs and actions of adherents. Because plausibility structures provide the background and framework for individuals' beliefs and behaviors, a change introduced to a given plausibility structure by a recognized leader of that plausibility structure will necessarily affect what is considered plausible. This research will help us understand the interdynamics of plausibility structural change, first of pastors, and the new behavior of adherents (laity) and the problem this creates for laity.

As long as a person's actions are consistent with his/her plausibility structure, there is no discrepancy between one's actions and values. But if there is a discrepancy between a person's actions and his/her plausibility structure, we see that there is a serious discrepancy between his/her actions and values. As a result of this discrepancy, one of three things should take place:

1) the person must cease the activity which is discrepant with the plausibility structure,

2) the person must add a cognitive element which will incorporate the new action— this may be difficult to accomplish in a firm and tightly constructed plausibility structure which disapproves of the action at the outset, or

3) the person can remove herself/himself from that plausibility structure altogether so as to avoid providing defenses of the action in question. By associating with those "who feel as I do," it is easier to continue a new form of action and to adopt the values making the action in question not only "plausible" but necessary.

Chapter Five

Social Mobility And Plausibility Structures

Social Location and Social Activism

What is the relationship of social location to social action among fundamentalists? If the fundamentalist engagement in social activism of the last decade is due to a rise in the social location of fundamentalists, we may perceive social action behavior to be a result of associating with peers outside of the fundamentalist plausibility structure, thus weakening the plausibility structure's hold on them. Belonging to professional occupations, acquiring higher educational degrees and having the economic resources to extend oneself beyond one's immediate plausibility structure serves to increase one's interaction and openness to views and lifestyles other than one's own. Fundamentalists' increased resources, power, and respectability since World War II would affect the plausibility of certain fundamentalist values such as social separatism. A rise in socioeconomic status could well obviate the need for maintaining separation from society at large.

Historical and sociological literature have demonstrated a relationship between social mobility and religiosity (Weber, 1958; Niebuhr, 1929; Lenski, 1963; Pope, 1942). Building on Weber's idea that religiosity can influence social mobility by encouraging thrift, hard work and asceticism, contemporary sociologists have demonstrated that upward mobility has been part of the American experience for many religious groups (e.g. Demerath, 1965; Niebuhr, 1929).

Social mobility involves the assumption of a social hierarchy along which mobility may occur. Evidences of upward mobility include increased wealth, more desirable occupational status, better education and changes in groups of association (Kohn, 1977). Social mobility has been known to disrupt established forms of social behavior and to have potent religio-psychological consequences (Goldthorpe, 1980). The rise in education, income and occupational status of fundamentalists in the last decades appears to have provided the large corps of activists and resources for the New Christian Right (Guth, 1983) and has influenced fundamentalists to adopt social action behavior, and at least for clergy, social action values (see Chapter Six).

Verba and Nie (1972) make it clear that citizens of higher social and economic status participate more in politics. This seems to hold true whether one uses educational level, income or occupation as the measure of social status. Economic, political and occupational stratification are "closely intercorrelated" with each other. Those who occupy the upper strata in one respect also tend to be in the upper strata in other respects and vice versa. The general rule is that "the poor are politically disfranchised and dwell in the lowest strata of the occupational hierarchy" (Sorokin, 1965:571).

Here we are concerned with the relation of social mobility to fundamentalists' recent involvement in social action. We expect that the effects of social mobility tend to disturb rather than to maintain one's ties to the fundamentalist plausibility structure. Since occupations are highly correlated to wealth and prestige, movement from one occupational category to another by generations should indicate the amount of social mobility occurring from one generation to the next.

In keeping with the upwardly mobile trend, fundamentalism has not only achieved middle class status, but has become an acceptable label to many Christians. Jerry Falwell made it clear in 1981 that he was at that time proud to be labelled a "fundamentalist." Co-founder of the Moral Majority, Greg Dixon, and innumerable other Moral Majority pastors are also proud to be called fundamentalists.

It has been noted in the past that as fundamentalists' socioeconomic status has improved, extremes of emotional expression have tended to moderate somewhat and communal involvement has increased (Perry, 1959; also cf. Verba and Nie, 1972). The separatist stance toward society has in many cases given way to involvement in mainstream American thinking (Niebuhr, 1929; Perry, 1959). In the middle class suburban church, orthodoxy in economic theory and politics has often been noted to become more important than orthodox theology. The fundamentalism which originally was concerned with soul salvation could be in danger of being transformed into an interest in economics, politics and social behavior. This transformation is consistent with church-sect theory as outlined by Troeltsch (1931) and H. Richard Niebuhr (1929) in the sense that group interests broaden as they gain wealth and prestige. Perry (1959) believes that the object of protest tends to move from the specifically theological to the economic as one experiences socioeconomic mobility.

However, in relation to the fundamentalism of a Jerry Falwell or Greg Dixon, it is not clear whether this is the case. Being a Christian "witness" is clearly a high priority item. Yet it is clear that maximizing power and influence both privately and publicly are also concerns of both Falwell and Dixon. I don't think for one minute we should doubt the cruciality of doctrinal beliefs and Christian dedication of these fundamentalist leaders. Religious dedication is what shapes the character of fundamentalism.

There are those who maintain that social mobility and its accompanying social power need not be a dissociative phenomenon which necessarily leads to the disruption of primary social relations. A widening in the individual's range of social relationships and activities may actually be the most probable outcome (Goldthorpe, 263). We have seen Falwell's abrasiveness tone down since the inception of the Moral Majority. He has retracted things he said and has purportedly moved from "hating the homosexual" to "hating homosexuality." He has repented of castigating Martin Luther King Jr. for his civil rights activities, he has repented of his promise never to get involved in politics. He is now claiming to be evangelical. While he once preached that Jews were going to hell, today he speaks in synagogues and has said the following:

> God has blessed America because we have blessed the Jews....The Jews look on conservative Christianity as the right wing that has been their enemy in years past. It is only a modern phenomenon that conservative Christianity is pro-Jewish (*Christianity Today*, September 21, 1981).

In 1982 the Southern Baptist Convention supported the call to allow voluntary prayer in government schools. They were roundly criticized by some for abandoning their previous adherence to strict separationism between church and state. The criticism is formally correct, but the change may have more to do with change of status. A religious community that no longer understands itself as an embattled minority begins to think more about influence than tolerance (Neuhaus, 1984:40).

Oftentimes a change in religious affiliation and orientation accompanies upward mobility (Niebuhr, 1929; Demerath, 1965). If an individual's socioeconomic status rises more quickly than his or her denomination's social status, the individual may leave the denomination. In comparison to the social mobility of the denomination as a whole, the individual can rise much faster. Witness the many lay persons and clergy who start out identifying with fundamentalism but eventually affiliate with non-fundamentalist churches and institutions (cf. Stark and Glock, 1968). Though not a fundamentalist, Oral Roberts' move from the Pentecostal Holiness sect to United Methodism is a example of this sort of phenomenon. It seems that the classical Pentecostal had "outgrown" the sub-cultural milieu that Pentecostalism offered and/or did not wish to put up with the behavioral constraints of the Pentecostal cultural milieu. The "respectability" of a mainline denomination became appealing as he desired a broader support base. Applied to fundamentalism, one may consider fundamentalism to involve more primitive processes of socialization; as the individual moves up the scale of a social hierarchy, he or she advances to more sophisticated social processes and interaction (cf. Stark and Glock, 1968).

Besides encouraging upwardly mobile individuals to leave fundamentalism for the older, wealthier and more prestigious denominations, the process of intergenerational mobility—movement up the social scale within a person's own lifetime—serves to socialize these individuals into mainstream thinking. It also socializes them to mainstream values. Because social and economic sophistication has become more of a reality, feelings of economic deprivation (as relative as they may be) no longer need to be assuaged. People are more comfortable with persons of the same socioeconomic standing. Perhaps they are even using the new religious affiliation to reinforce their upward social mobility. Though the idea of widespread denominational switching as one rises socioeconomically is contested by some sociologists (e.g. Nelson and Snizek, 1976), there is evidence to support the fact that people often do change denominations as they rise socioeconomically (Newport, 1979; Demerath, 1965; Roberts, 1984; Kelley, 1972). While the mainline denominations appear to be losing more members than they are gaining, members tend to drop out of the church altogether as opposed to switching to more conservative denominations, though there are those who do the latter (cf. Keith Roberts, 1984). As upwardly mobile individuals become accommodated to the larger society, the respective religious movement proceeds to accommodate itself too, but in a slower fashion (Glock, 1973:209).

Upward mobility of individuals within fundamentalism can filter members and leadership of fundamentalists into non-fundamentalist denominations and organizations. This loss of members and leaders may contribute to incoherency and disorganization (cf. Lefever, 1984) rather than to the institutional growth of fundamentalist churches. Upward social mobility of individuals is likely to lead them into contact with different institutions and people in society—and these contacts weaken their attachments to the fundamentalist plausibility structure.

Denominations as a whole can also rise vertically. H. Richard Niebuhr (1929) pointed out the effects on sects and denominations alike of rapid movement from frontier to urban industrial society. For example, old-line groups such as the Methodists and Baptists which began as sects have experienced rapid vertical mobility resulting in their evolving into denominations. Their rise in social status has provided a basis upon which fundamentalist sects could sprout and eventually rise to denominational status themselves. The upward mobility of sects to middle class respectability has contributed greatly to the persistence of fundamentalism in that fundamentalism is continually fed by people who "move up" from smaller and more extreme sects. Missions, Bible schools and church building keep fundamentalist numbers from dwindling and ensure that the fundamentalist orientation continues (Kelley, 1972, 1984). Also, the sects are more serious in their attempts to convert the unchurched and thereby have a larger supply of new recruits than do the mainline church groups (cf. Kelley, 1972). While the fundamentalist movement may have been a reaction to specific historical occurrences in its origins, its persistence indicates that it now has roots in the continuing social processes of society (cf. Perry, 1959:186).

Fundamentalism has undergone both a consciously directed and a neutral institutionalization, taking on the general pattern of schools and churches which was its heritage. This institutionalization provided the framework for perpetuation. Certain features of the social order also produce continuing needs which fundamentalism supplies. The social class system means a continuing discrepancy in cultural attainment and contact with alternate strata in the social hierarchy. Some people inevitably will be alienated and/or frustrated in society. As long as there is social mobility, there will be dislocation of some individuals from community relationships producing recruits for fundamentalism and other social movements and institutions. The steady influx of recruits demonstrates to fundamentalist leaders and followers that the fundamentalist faith works. Continuing social and economic complexities also provide the demand for the simple solutions of fundamentalism.

Hence the ranks of fundamentalism may be continually resupplied as higher socioeconomic members are filtered into the more established and more prestigious denominations.

Hypotheses

The hypotheses tested in this section concern the relation of social location to one's adherence to the plausibility structures.

5.1   Intergenerational change of social status is inversely related to the
       strength of one's ties to the fundamentalist plausibility structure.

I expect those fundamentalist believers who have experienced intergenerational change of social status to have loosened their ties to the traditional fundamentalist plausibility structure. Hence they may have exchanged many fundamentalist ideas for ideas more compatible with their new plausibility structure.

5.2   Intergenerational change in social status is positively correlated with
       the strength of one's ties to the Moral Majority plausibility structure.

A change in social status should serve to increase the integration of people into the larger society (Verba and Nie, 1972). Pertaining to fundamentalist Christians, one should expect that those experiencing intergenerational rise in social status to be more socially active and hence more prone to engage in and support Moral Majority activities than those with little or no intergenerational rise in social status. There should be less need for upwardly mobile fundamentalists to keep the protectionist stance anchored in the fundamentalist plausibility structure.

To test hypotheses 5.1 and 5.2, two regression models were used. In the first model, ties to the plausibility structures are regressed on origination (father's education) and destination (respondent's education) effects. In the second model, ties to the plausibility structures are regressed on origination, destination and interaction (respondent's education minus father's education) effects. The reason for comparing additive versus interactive models is to see what effects mobility per se of the respondent has on allegiance to plausibility structures. This method for testing mobility per se is fully outlined in Knoke (1973). Respondents who are socially mobile often retain values and attitudes of their parents and social class (origination effects). Yet they also adopt many characteristics, values and attitudes of the social group which they join through upward social mobility (destination effects). In order to isolate the impact of social mobility itself on the respondent, we add an interaction term which consists of respondent's education (destination) minus father's education (origination). This interaction term allows us to test the influence of social mobility against the additive effects of origination and destination effects.

Table 5.1

EFFECTS OF INTERGENERATIONAL CHANGE OF STATUS ON PLAUSIBILITY STRUCTURES

Fundamentalist Plausibility Structure

Clergy:

$$FPS = 4.5 + .0009Y + .19Z$$

$$R^2 = .01 \qquad \begin{array}{l} EQ.\ 5.1 \\ F = 1.2 \end{array} \quad S = .30$$

$$FPS = 4.5 - .02Y + .21Z - .021$$

$$R^2 = .00 \qquad \begin{array}{l} EQ.\ 5.2 \\ F = .80 \end{array} \quad S = .50$$

Laity:

$$FPS = 5.0 - .06Y + .12Z**$$

$$R^2 = .05 \qquad \begin{array}{l} EQ.\ 5.3 \\ F = 3.3 \end{array} \quad S = .04$$

$$FPS = 5.0 - .11Y + .17Z - .05I$$

$$R^2 = .04 \qquad \begin{array}{l} EQ.\ 5.4 \\ F = 2.2 \end{array} \quad S = .10$$

Moral Majority Plausibility Structure

Clergy:

$$MMPS = 12.3 - .74Y* - .05Z$$

$$R^2 = .08 \qquad \begin{array}{l} EQ.\ 5.5 \\ F = 2.4 \end{array} \quad S = .11$$

$$MMPS = 12.5 + 2.8Y - 3.3Z + 3.2I$$

$$R^2 = .11 \qquad \begin{array}{l} EQ.\ 5.6 \\ F = 2.3 \end{array} \quad S = .10$$

Laity:

$$MMPS = 9.8 + .57Y** - .89**$$

$$R^2 = .14 \qquad \begin{array}{l} EQ.\ 5.7 \\ F = 5.7 \end{array} \quad S = .005$$

$$MMPS = 11.1 + 2.8Y*** - 3.3Z*** + 2.31**$$

$$R^2 = .23 \qquad \begin{array}{l} EQ.\ 5.8 \\ F = 6.9 \end{array} \quad S = .001$$

* probability < .05   ** probability < .01
*** probability < .001

where:

   FPS   = Fundamentalist Plausibility Structure
   MMPS   = Moral Majority Plausibility Structure
   Y   = Father's Educational Status
   Z   = Respondent's Educational Status
   I   = Interaction Effects (respondent's education minus father's
             education with a one year difference set equal to zero to
             avoid linear dependency).

Equations 5.1 and 5.2 demonstrate that intergenerational change of status has little effect on clergy ties to the fundamentalist plausibility structure in either the additive or interactive models. Findings are slightly different for laity. Equation 5.3 indicates that the respondent's educational level causes lay members to be attached to the fundamentalist plausibility structure. In Equation 5.4 respondent's education loses significance due to multicollinearity of respondent's education and the interaction measure (respondent's education minus father's education). In this case we reject the interactive model.

Equation 5.5 demonstrates that father's educational status is negatively related to clergy ties to the Moral Majority plausibility structure. Origination effects seem to predict clergy ties to the Moral Majority plausibility structure better than destination effects. By testing the adjusted $R2$'s of Equations 5.5 and 5.6 through the fundamentalist ratio, we see that the interaction model does not explain a significantly larger proportion of the variance than the additive model. In the interactive model, father's education also loses significance due to multicollinearity of father's education with the interaction measure. We accept the additive model in this case because the negative impact of father's education helps to explain clergy ties to the Moral Majority plausibility structure whereas the interactive model gives no significant information. For laity, the interactive model explains a significantly larger proportion of the variance than the additive model at the .05 level. When the interaction term is added in Equation 5.8, father's education and respondent's education become even more significant than they are in the additive model (Equation 5.7). The interaction term is also significant. Father's education is positively related to ties of the laity to the Moral Majority plausibility structure whereas respondent's educational level is negatively related to their ties to the Moral

Majority plausibility structure. The interaction term is positively related to respondent's ties to the Moral Majority plausibility structure meaning that the more a respondent's education exceeds the father's education, the greater the respondent's ties to the Moral Majority plausibility structure.

In sum, Equations 5.1 and 5.2 indicate that the analysis of intergenerational change of status does not provide an adequate explanation of clergy ties to the fundamentalist plausibility structure. However, Equation 5.5 indicates that father's educational status tends to predict clergy ties to the Moral Majority plausibility structure via its negative net effect. Intergenerational change of status does a better job at predicting ties to the plausibility structures for laity. Respondent's educational status is positively related to ties of the laity to the fundamentalist plausibility structure (Equation 5.4) and negatively related to ties of the laity to the Moral Majority plausibility structure (Equation 5.8). Father's educational level is related to ties of the laity to the Moral Majority plausibility structure and social mobility per se also effects ties of the laity to the Moral Majority plausibility structure. Hypotheses 5.1 is not supported. Intergenerational change of status is not inversely related to strength of ties to the fundamentalist plausibility structure. Hypotheses 5.2 is not supported for clergy but is for laity. Social mobility per se has an independent positive effect on lay members' ties to the Moral Majority plausibility structure.

In correlating current socioeconomic status to plausibility structures we again see no influence of socioeconomic status on plausibility structure for clergy, but see a significant effect of socioeconomic status on lay members' ties to the fundamentalist plausibility structure. This is consistent with Equations 5.2 and 5.4 above.

Discussion

One explanation for the lack of inverse relation between fundamentalist plausibility structure and intergenerational change in social status may lie in the rapid vertical mobility which some people have experienced in America. Because some people move from comparative poverty to wealth in less than a lifetime, this does not mean that they move as rapidly in social comprehension or awareness.

Persons moving upward in the social class hierarchy may bring their former cultural background and religious orientation to the new economic level (Perry, 1959:116). In other words, there may be a time lag in one's understanding or growth in human knowledge and experience as compared to their growth in wealth. William Ogburn (1932) clearly outlines how part of one's culture may not change at the same rate as others, though there is generally a correlation and an interdependency of parts. Changes in material culture tend to precede changes in adaptive culture. In this sense, economic mobility would occur first and sociopolitical outlook may eventually follow (Ogburn, 1932:1273). "Unchanged adaptive culture is more harmoniously related to the old than to the new material condition and a new adaptive culture will be better suited to the new material conditions than was the old adaptive culture. Adjustment is a relative term and there are few cases of perfect adjustment" (Ogburn, 1932:1273).

Perry describes cases where businessmen progressed economically so rapidly that the old-time statements of Christian responsibility remained applicable only to "individual salvation and philanthropy" (Perry, 1959:120). It is conceivable that a person well grounded in such a worldview could be immune to the influences of outside experience as he or she rises socioeconomically. In this case, one would expect ties to fundamentalism to remain rigid and intact.

Marsden (1980) maintains that fundamentalists' religious and political ideals hardened "at about the point they had reached by 1900." If this is so, then rigid ties to the fundamentalist plausibility structure could indeed keep one from "growing" or expanding one's worldview as the entire fundamentalist movement progressed socioeconomically.

It appears that fathers with more education may have taught their offspring to be more aware and involved socially than fathers with less education. The significant effect of social mobility on lay ties to the Moral Majority plausibility structure offers substance to hypothesis 5.2 that a rise in social status serves to increase the integration of people into the larger society. These may be the Moral Majoritarians who have less need for keeping the protectionist stance that is anchored in the fundamentalist plausibility structure.

An explanation for the positive relationship between socioeconomic status and fundamentalist plausibility structure for laity may be that those who have achieved a degree of socioeconomic status wish to secure their place in an uncertain world. Remembering what it is like to have less than they do, their educational and implicit financial gain may serve to strengthen their ties to a plausibility structure that has proven to *work* for them. They may interpret their gain to be a result of God's blessings, and respond by increasing their devotion to a system that works. However, we can say that the fact that laity of some degree of social standing are tightly bonded to the fundamentalist plausibility structure demonstrates that the relationship between fundamentalism and the lower socioeconomic strata is not an exclusive one.

Table 5.2
CORRELATIONS OF SOCIAL STATUS AND PLAUSIBILITY STRUCTURE

Socio-economic Status	Ties to Fundamentalist Plausibility Structure	Ties to Moral Majority Plausibility Structure
Clergy	.27	.24
Laity	.32**	-.22

** probability < .01

According to Table 5.4, clergy ties to plausibility structures are seemingly unaffected by socioeconomic status. Though more involved in society, clergy appear to be unaffected by socioeconomic influences in this sample. This is most likely the case because their remuneration does not reflect their responsibilities or educational attainment.

Socioeconomic status plays a more important role for ties of the laity to the fundamentalist plausibility structure than it does for clergy. This may be due to the fact that educational attainment is not paying off for clergy as it is for laypersons.

While the correlation between income and education is .25 at the .01 level of significance for laity, it is only .03 and insignificant for clergy.

In Chapter Six we will see how clergy and laity respond differently in terms of social action and social action values. From Table 5.4 we can already expect laity to have significantly lower levels of social action values than clergy due to the fact they have stronger ties to the fundamentalist plausibility structure than the Moral Majority plausibility structure.

Chapter Six

Social Action And Social Action Values

Ever since Max Weber's distinction between religions whose goals were "this worldly" or "other worldly" and those whose actions tended to be "mystical" or "ascetic," different religious systems have been known to have different consequences for social beliefs and actions. For example, the varieties of Protestant denominations have different ethical implications in terms of social actions and values. What a person holds to be true and what behaviors he or she engages in are in many ways dependent upon the religious cultural complex (broadly speaking) or, more specifically, the plausibility structure a person finds oneself in. Troeltsch (1931) clustered dimensions of religious groups under two polarities in a sect-church continuum. Weber classified according to a traditional-rational continuum. Driedger et al. (1983) classifies according to Wuthnow's dualist-holist perspective. Wuthnow (1981) finds that the lines of division in the study of religion are a cleavage between two competing epistemological orientations derived from Cartesian dualism and holistic phenomenology. In applying the dualistic-holistic perspective to religious adherents, Driedger et al. state that fundamentalists hold to a more dualist view of God and God's dealings with men than do liberals, and they also have a more dualist view of the Christian community than liberals do (cf. Driedger et al.: 225). The question is whether the church should identify with society as the "church" does in the Troeltschian sense, or remain apart and critique society as the sect does (Troeltsch, 1931).

While the dualistic tradition emphasizes belief and cognition, the holistic tradition focuses more on symbols. Driedger et al. suggest that members of the Christian religion tend to view God, man, and the world from these two epistemological orientations. Correspondingly, those with a dualist worldview will be concerned with different social problems and issues than those with a holistic perspective (1983:228).

> Theologically dualists (especially fundamentalists) seem to see Theos as transcendent or other worldly. The world is viewed as corrupt, and humans must be rescued from the clutches of sin into the realm of the transcendent supernatural...in contrast, holists see God as imminent, working and changing the world, and concerned with issues of the day. Fundamentalist belief in miracles, the virgin birth of Christ, and the inerrancy of Scriptures are usually cast in dualist, black and white, terms that set them apart from the natural processes of society (228).

Consequently, dualists are likely to support issues of personal morality, and they will be concerned with the social control of deviants, and less concerned with the larger societal issues of the power elite and the rights and welfare of others (Wuthnow, 1973; Dreidger et al., 1983). They will be more preoccupied with the survival of their own beliefs and group.

Falwell's excuse for the Moral Majority's not helping the poor (see *Christianity Today*, 1981; also see Chapter Two) fits in here. His focus is on survival of fundamentalist rights, values and the Moral Majority as opposed to helping "outsiders." An exception to this observation is the program of helping unwed pregnant women. The criticism often leveled here is that these homes for unwed mothers in many states may put pressure on them to convert. So in this sense the social aid still benefits the fundamentalist program of soul salvation. It would seem that the development of a program for AIDS victims would be more likely to invalidate the role of fundamentalist interest in social endeavors. Helping "outsiders" is more likely to be on the agenda of liberal Christians who have not—at least until the Moral Majority came on the scene—had to be concerned with their survival. A more liberal theological perspective will be less preoccupied with purely personal morality but will be more interested in issues and problems of human liberty, social welfare, and the like.

While there has been considerable research on social activism among liberal Protestant denominations (i.e., Quinley, 1974; Hadden, 1970; Hadden and Longino, 1974; Stark et al. 1973; Wood, 1981), relatively little research has been conducted on social action in the more conservative Protestant denominations.

Today we have a proliferation of fundamentalist conservative social action organizations such as Christian Voice, Religious Roundtable, Bill Bright's Campus Crusade for Christ, Third Century Publishers, American Christian Cause, National Christian Action Coalition and the Moral Majority, among others. We have been inundated with books and articles covering the many aspects of the New Christian Right. While conservative political organizations have proliferated on the political horizon, conservative denominations by and large still have chosen to remain in the background of the sociopolitical arena. However, there is some involvement at the transdenominational level. Jerry Falwell claims that the Moral Majority is not a religious, but a *political* organization. He has contributed to the notion that churches and religious organizations have no role in the "naked public square" (cf. Neuhaus, 1984). Though this is questionable when considering his role in the public arena, his public actions support this notion. In this way he can mix church and state relations without being technically "guilty" of doing so. (Perhaps he is forced into this form of hypocrisy by the forum already staged in the Public Square. He is merely playing by the rules set by society.)

The New Christian Right has distinguished itself from Old Conservatism by its tactics rather than its political ideology (see Chapter Two). The New Christian Right is well known for having tremendously sophisticated mailing strategies and electronic media facilities such as the machinery set in motion by Richard Viguery. What kind of social action behaviors are the grass roots following of the New Christian Right groups encouraged to take? What are their methods of "activism"? How radical are conservatives allowed to get in the name of conservative causes?

This study of the Moral Majority can help answer these questions. Clearly, certain social action behaviors are more acceptable to Moral Majoritarians than others, maybe even more "moral." Fundamentalist social and political views are products of fundamentalist theology. Fundamentalists are passionate about social and political matters precisely because they are passionate about theology (Hadden and Swann, 1981). In fact, it's difficult to find many areas within a fundamentalist's life where he/she is not impassioned. They believe that their positions are totally biblical and can quote biblical texts to prove every point. This moral certitude is offensive to many evangelicals and is one item that distinguishes fundamentalists from evangelicals. Once we pass over the breach in fundamentalist policy against social activism, we can see that, indeed, Moral Majority social activism *is* intrinsically related to their theological views. I asked the Reverend Greg Dixon, former National Secretary for the Moral Majority and former Chairman of the Indiana chapter, the following questions regarding the relation of social action to the Christian message: "Are most of the social action issues that the Moral Majority is involved in related to the Christian message or morality? What social actions wouldn't the Moral Majority get involved in?" Dixon responded:

> There aren't too many areas unconcerned with morality. The goal of the Moral Majority is not to Christianize America though it is the goal of Roman Catholicism, but our goal is to preach, evangelize, and maintain liberties under the Constitution so that the Gospel may continue to be preached and our liberties maintained. We want to 'occupy until Christ returns.' I believe the return of Christ is imminent. We must work as if he will come in our lifetime, but plan as if he will not. The Christian must rejoice and weep at the same time. It pains you deeply to see when the nation goes wrong but we rejoice because our redemption draweth nigh.

When I asked Dixon what mechanisms the Moral Majority advocated for social change, he replied that democratic methods, such as voting, were the best methods of social activism. My data indicate that other kinds of acceptable social action behaviors include giving money to political candidates and/or parties, petitioning, boycotting, rallying, writing legislators and congressmen, marching quietly and, to a lesser extent, staging mass demonstrations with large crowds of people.

Social action behaviors considered to be less appropriate include staging "sit-ins" or "walk-outs," engaging in civil disobedience, breaking laws which are considered unjust and taking part in strikes and pickets. These kinds of social action behaviors generally are considered to be too radical, if not unchristian, by Moral Majoritarians. They also depend on collective action such as unionized activities rather than one's individual ideological commitment. However, the social psychological tactics used by the leadership of the Moral Majority to mobilize its constituency to engage in social activism is of a different nature and will be discussed in Chapter Seven.

Table 6.1
ATTITUDES TOWARD SOCIAL ACTION

	Yes	No
1. Take action such as either boycotting or getting up a petition.	96% (n=136)	3% (n=5)
2. Hold public speeches and rallies.	92% (n=129)	8% (n=11)
3. Stage mass demonstrations with large crowds of people.	65% (n= 87)	35% (n=46)
4. Engage in civil disobedience by breaking laws which are considered unjust.	7% (n= 10)	92% (n=123)
5. Take actions such as "sit-ins" or "walk-outs."	24% (n= 31)	76% (n=98)
6. March quietly and peacefully through town.	82% (n=111)	18% (n=24)

As far as social action behaviors that Moral Majority members have actually engaged in, we get a similar picture. Following are frequencies of actual social action behaviors which Moral Majority respondents reportedly engaged in (see questions 112, 137-141 in Appendix D).

Table 6.2
SOCIAL ACTION BEHAVIOR

	Yes	No
1. Have you ever given money to support a political candidate?	63% (n=98)	37% (n=57)
2. Have you ever donated money to a political organization?	58% (n=90)	42% (n=64)
3. Have you ever taken part in a strike?	11% (n=17)	89% (n=139)
4. Have you ever made a phone call to protest a certain social action?	71% (n=110)	29% (n=45)
5. Have you ever been in a picket line?	14% (n=42)	86% (n=134)

These findings indicate that striking and picketing are responded to differently than other types of social action behavior listed in Table 6.2. Unlike the other self-initiated and low-cost actions, striking and picketing depend more heavily upon other persons' joint actions as well as the opportunity to engage in such activities. For instance, strikes are collective actions that not only depend on having a good job, but depend on one's working in a unionized industry or having disrupted negotiations. The likelihood that all of these circumstances will fall into place is cumulatively much lower than the simple action of donating money or making a phone call.

The social action possibilities of the Moral Majority constituency tend to be limited to safe, democratic means and do not tend to be of a radical nature that were more typical of some counterculture groups of the sixties for example. Moral Majoritarians, as most New Christian Right groups, prefer to work within the given political system rather than staging onslaughts against it.

Social Action Since the Moral Majority

About the time of the 1980 presidential election, the news media attacked right-wing radicals such as Falwell for instigating a Nazi, fascist mentality and position. Books came off the press warning of the potential danger of new Christian Right groups, and in particular, the Moral Majority (Shriver, 1981; Kater, 1982; Jorstad, 1981; Hadden and Swann, 1981; McIntyre, 1979; Webber, 1981). After Reagan won the presidential nomination and liberal commentators and scholars had a chance to reevaluate the impact of the New Christian Right, many concluded that right wing groups such as the Moral Majority actually had far less sway than formerly thought (Hadden and Swann, 1981). Instead of being feared for their awesome power in the political arena, New Right groups were often looked upon with disdain for claiming to have wielded more political clout and power than they actually did.

To what extent has the Moral Majority activated its members to social action? How effective has the Moral Majority been in activating members to rally to its cause? As an indication of being mobilized to social activism, respondents were asked whether they first took the following action more than five years ago, less than five years ago, or whether they never took this action (see questions 28-31 in Appendix D).

Table 6.3
SOCIAL ACTION INVOLVEMENT SINCE
THE FOUNDING OF THE MORAL MAJORITY

		Never Took Action	Took Action Less than 5 Years Ago	Took Action More than 5 Years Ago
1.	Displayed an American flag at my home.	35% (n=56)	7% (n=12)	58% (n=94)
2.	Taken part in a rally against an immoral activity in my community.	41% (n=66)	25% (n=40)	35% (n=56)
3.	Written my congressman in support of a larger defense budget.	64% (n=104)	19% (n=30)	17% (n=28)
4.	Written my congressman on a foreign policy issue.	67% (n=108)	13% (n=21)	20% (n=33)

More respondents were activated in the last five years to take part in a rally than to display flags or to write congressmen. It seems that Jerry Falwell's "I Love America" rallies which took place on the steps of capitals of most states across the country may account for the largest percent of Moral Majoritarians engaging in this activity within the early eighties. Roy McLaughlin, Chairman of the Arkansas Chapter of the Moral Majority, claimed in a recent interview that he could stage a rally of about 5,000 persons on the steps of the Arkansas state capitol within three days. Staging rallies seems to be one of the most effective forms of social action the Moral Majority has utilized for gaining recognition. Rallies are highly visible. Born-again Christians with little experience in social activism can easily follow the leadership of the Moral Majority into this activity without much personal preparation other than physical presence.

Displaying flags at one's home may not be considered as "social action" in the same sense that writing legislators or rallying is. It has the smallest increase over the last five years than the other types of social action. It also has the largest number of respondents involved before the last five years. Letter writing as a tool to influence legislation has increased significantly in the last five years, especially in regard to a larger defense budget. Maintaining national security through a strong military defense is, of course, one of the most important platforms of the Moral Majority.

Table 6.4*
COMPOSITE ACTION

	Never Took Action	Acted in Last 5 Years	Acted Before 5 Years
Clergy	9% (n=4)	55% (n=26)	77% (n=36)
Laity	10% (n=9)	48% (n=43)	67% (n=60)

Table 6.4 shows that 9% of the clergy (n=4) and 10% of the laity (n=9) NEVER took part in any of the actions described in Table 6.3. Fifty-five percent of the clergy (n=26) and 48% of the laity (n=43) FIRST took part in one of the actions in the last five years. This is a good indication of the influence that the Moral Majority may have had on members. Seventy-seven percent of the clergy (n=36) and 67% of the laity (n=60) had taken part in one of these actions previous to the last five years.

---

* Figures in Table 6.4 should not necessarily add up to 100%. Some respondents undoubtedly will have taken some actions within the last five years while partaking in other actions before the last five years, hence scoring in two columns.

Because of the effect of the Moral Majority on its constituency, I hypothesize a Moral Majority plausibility structure that is separate and distinct from the traditional fundamentalist plausibility structure.

Hypotheses

Research hypotheses for this section are stated as follows:

6.1   Strength of ties to the Moral Majority plausibility structure is correlated with engagement in social action behaviors.

We can see that the Moral Majority appears to have been instrumental in instigating social action among members. Verba and Nie (1972) demonstrate that one reason citizens may participate in political life is because of their affiliation with an organization. Organizational affiliation has been shown to be one of the most powerful predictors of citizen activity—even stronger than the impact of social class on the individual (Verba and Nie, 1972). Therefore, in this case, the more ties one has to the Moral Majority plausibility structure, the more one is expected to take part in social action behaviors.

6.2   Strength of ties to the fundamentalist plausibility structure is inversely correlated to engagement in social action behaviors.

The fundamentalist plausibility structure has traditionally not supported social action of its members. There are numerous reasons for expecting ties to the fundamentalist plausibility structure to be inversely related to social action behaviors (see Chapter One).

6.3   Ties to the fundamentalist plausibility structure will be negatively related to ties to the Moral Majority plausibility structure.

A negative relationship is expected between the two plausibility structures due to their opposing stresses on social action. The fundamentalist plausibility structure supports evangelism at the expense of social action, but the Moral Majority plausibility structure supports social action without regard to evangelism.

6.3.1 This inverse relationship between plausibility structures is due to the opposing stresses that each plausibility structure places on social action. The Moral Majority plausibility structure is positively related to social action whereas the fundamentalist plausibility structure is negatively related to social action.

Table 6.5
SOCIAL ACTION AND PLAUSIBILITY STRUCTURES

Social Action	Ties to Moral Majority Plausibility Structure	Ties to Fundamentalist Plausibility Structure
Clergy	.29*	.07
Laity	.33*	-.04
Social Action Values		
Clergy	.29*	.01
Laity	.09	-.31**

* Probability < .05   ** Probability < .01

Hypotheses 6.1, that ties to the Moral Majority plausibility structure are correlated with engagement in social action, is supported. The Moral Majority plausibility structure is indeed correlated to engagement in social action activities for laity as well as clergy, though the relationship is somewhat stronger for laity.

Results do not support hypothesis 6.2, that there is an inverse correlation of the fundamentalist plausibility structure to engagement in social action. While ties to the fundamentalist plausibility structure certainly are not promoting social action endeavors, they are social action values that clearly demonstrate the inverse relationship with the fundamentalist plausibility structure. But this inverse relationship holds only for laity. Analysis indicates that the Moral Majority plausibility structure is significantly correlated with social action values for clergy, but not laity. However, a negative relation does exist between social action values and the fundamentalist plausibility structure for laity. Clergy with strong ties to the Moral Majority plausibility structure have social action values and laypersons with strong ties to the fundamentalist plausibility structure have anti-social action values. It is intriguing that while laypersons attached to the Moral Majority plausibility structure do not have strong social action *values*, they do nonetheless demonstrate the social action *behaviors* expected of Moral Majoritarians. This may be evidence of leadership influence and laymember's susceptibility to that influence. According to Wood (1981), religious laypersons may accept and support policies that they personally disapprove of and would not have supported by themselves. In the case of the Moral Majority, not only do members support policies that they may not have done on their own initiative, they even participate in actions that do not fit into their cognitive schema of values.

Leaders of a movement seem to be more likely to hold to the "core values" of a given organization than laymembers (Wood, 1981). In this sense, clergymen should be expected to be more supportive of Moral Majority thinking and values regardless of their rise in social status while laypersons would be more expected to follow pastor's leads and directives whether or not they agreed with them. These laypersons may be following their pastors' lead by joining the Moral Majority organization and even by engaging in social action supported by the Moral Majority. If laypersons are following their pastor's lead, they would not necessarily have adopted the values and cognitive framework that are supportive of social action and the Moral Majority platform.

One can expect Moral Majoritarians who have strong ties to the fundamentalist plausibility structure to experience a certain degree of cognitive dissonance because while they have not yet adopted the social action *values* that the Moral Majority encourages, they are engaging in the social action *behaviors* that are supported by the Moral Majority. These laypersons may be in a transitory stage; while engaging in social action behaviors, they are developing those social values that would be consistent with social action. The process is not completed as yet. In a cross-sectional study such as this, a researcher must make allowances for transitions that could better be picked up through a longitudinal study. This issue will be further addressed in Chapter Seven.

Table 6.6
RELATIONSHIP OF TWO PLAUSIBILITY STRUCTURES

Ties to Moral Majority Plausibility Structure	Ties to Fundamentalist Plausibility Structure
Clergy	-.03
Laity	-.27***

*** Probability < .001

Findings in Table 6.6 provide limited support for hypothesis 6.3 that ties to the fundamentalist plausibility structure are inversely correlated with ties to the Moral Majority plausibility structure. The negative correlation is significant only for laity. This clearly demonstrates that laity are not likely to have ties to both the fundamentalist and the Moral Majority plausibility structures. Clergy may have ties to both, but apparently not the laity. This has serious implications as to who is likely to experience cognitive dissonance because of social action involvement.

Hypotheses 6.3.1 that the inverse relationship between plausibility structure is due to the opposing stresses that each place on social action is supported. Table 6.5 clearly indicates that the Moral Majority plausibility structure is significantly related to social action whereas the fundamentalist plausibility structure is not. Table 6.6 demonstrates that, at least for laity, a strong inverse relationship exists between plausibility structures. This difference in magnitude is probably due to the fact that laity are less sophisticated at rationalizing the opposing stances of the two plausibility structures regarding social action than clergy are. Moral Majority clergy must deal more with the two "conversational fabrics" than laypersons do and hence may better be able to legitimize both stances at once. Laity whose exposure to the Moral Majority is more likely to be limited than that of clergy would not easily facilitate two opposing views or operational networks. Previous research indicates that laypersons had more cross-cutting social attachments than clergy and hence were not as devoted to the "core values" of the church (Wood, 1981, 1984). However, in this study it appears that it is the clergy that may have more wide-ranging social attachments than laity and hence find less of a contradiction between the two plausibility structures than do laity. Consistent with Wood's findings, however, is that ministers have more liberal attitudes than members (Wood, 1981). Table 6.6 demonstrates that ties to the Moral Majority plausibility structure and fundamentalist plausibility structure inversely co-vary strongly for lay fundamentalists but not clergy. Laity may also be more susceptible to leadership direction, thus relying on pastors and Moral Majority leaders to provide needed rationales and direction for them. Laypersons may be more likely than clergy to follow leaders into activities and associations that they really do not agree with.

Susceptibility to Leadership

Leadership influence is an important element of a given plausibility structure and can have a great influence on the behavior and attitudes of the constituency of a given organization. It is through leadership that the goals of an organization are achieved (Wood, 1984). But what role does one's susceptibility to leadership play in causing a layperson to follow leadership direction? This section is especially pertinent to laity because they are the ones exposed to and expected to follow clergy or other leadership direction. I have hypothesized that:

6.4   There is an inverse relationship between susceptibility to leadership and socioeconomic status.

Those higher socioeconomically are expected to be less susceptible to leadership influence because they have more at stake in the outcome of the action in question. The higher-status individual has a greater stake in politics, has greater skills, more resources, greater awareness of political matters, is exposed to more communications about politics, and interacts with others who also participate (Verba and Nie, 1972). Individuals in the lower socioeconomic strata should be more expected to follow leadership direction because not only do they have less to lose, but they would be the more dissatisfied with their social condition and would have more to gain through change. Lipset (1963) maintains that the lower-class way of life produces individuals with rigid and intolerant outlooks. The resulting authoritarian personality tends to let leaders and ideologies serve as rigid guides to belief and behaviors. The authoritarian personality is also linked to those characteristics, attitudes, and predispositions which finds outlets in allegiance to extremist political movements (Lipset, 1963:100).[1]

6.5   There is an inverse relationship between susceptibility to leadership and ties to the fundamentalist plausibility structure.

Fundamentalists have been suspicious of leadership generally, especially leadership direction not aligned with their understanding and interpretation of Scripture and culture. Considering that socioeconomic status was positively correlated with the fundamentalist plausibility structure for laity (see Chapter Five), it is now reasonable to hypothesize that an inverse correlation ought to exist between susceptibility to leadership and fundamentalist plausibility structure, especially for laity.

6.6   There is a positive correlation between susceptibility to leadership and ties to the Moral Majority plausibility structure.

---

[1] Some scholars dispute the Lipset formulation that experiences within the working class are the sources of intolerance. For example, Richard F. Hamilton (1972) provides evidence that authoritarianism may come from without the working class due to farm-to-city movement and other migration patterns.

One would expect those more susceptible to leadership to be more open to a group like the Moral Majority who offers concrete direction, hope for political power, and influence of one's philosophical and economic interests. Those who are more enmeshed in the Moral Majority plausibility structure should be those more susceptible to the leadership influences of the Moral Majority.

Table 6.7
CORRELATIONS TO SUSCEPTIBILITY

Susceptibility to Leadership	Socioeconomic Status	Fundamentalist Plausibility Structure (controlling for SES)	Moral Majority Plausibility Structure (controlling for SES)
Laity	-.26*	-.89**	-.05
Clergy	-.09	.19	-.07

* Probability < .05 ** Probability < .01

Hypothesis 6.4 is supported. There is a significant inverse relation of susceptibility to leadership to socioeconomic status for laity. Having more economic resources, higher education and a more prestigious occupation serves to decrease one's susceptibility to leadership. Clergy are not affected in like manner. Perhaps this is because they are the "leaders" and consequently act more independently than laypersons. Also, as mentioned in Chapter Five, increased education is not paying off in terms of higher income for clergy as it is for laity. We do not have much socioeconomic variation for clergy of the Moral Majority in Indiana. Another interpretation is that lower status laypersons may believe in the legitimacy of clergy authority and depend on clergy for leadership and guidance whereas clergy may be content to retain that authority for themselves rather than looking to someone else such as Moral Majority or denominational officials for possible direction or guidance. Also, clergy may use their own sense of legitimate authority for claiming members' support (cf. Wood, 1981:68) or they may be appealing to traditional charisma of the prophets (Weber, 1964) for legitimation of their own authority. Both Greg Dixon and Jerry Falwell have pointed to the Hebrew prophets, Elijah, Micaiah, Nathan and others to legitimize their own behaviors and the social stances taken by the Moral Majority. But this is nothing new. The fundamentalist movement itself has based its authority on the charismatic style of the prophets. This emphasis on charisma and contact with God is one reason why education was originally considered to be a handicap rather than a tool for the early fundamentalist preacher. Education was seen to hinder one's openness to the leading of the Spirit of God (see Chapter One).

Hypotheses 6.5 is strongly supported (see Table 6.7). The more ties a layperson has to the fundamentalist plausibility structure, the less susceptible to leadership he or she is, even holding socioeconomic status constant. The fundamentalist mindset is generally unwavering in its loyalty to fundamentalist morals and values. Marsden (1980) speaks of the rigidity inherent in the fundamentalist mentality that defies explanation in purely economic or political terms (also cf. Kelley, 1984). And yet, some fundamentalists have been open to Moral Majority values and ideals, leading to weakened ties to the fundamentalist plausibility structure.

Hypotheses 6.6, that there is a positive correlation between susceptibility to leadership and ties to the Moral Majority plausibility structure is not supported. Those attracted to the Moral Majority are not necessarily those who require leadership assistance. We will have to look elsewhere for the underlying reasons for their cooperation with the Moral Majority.

Summary

In this chapter we found that having ties to the fundamentalist plausibility structure creates or sustains anti-social action values for laity but not for clergy. Having ties to the Moral Majority plausibility structure serves to predict social action behaviors for laity and for clergy, but having ties to the Moral Majority plausibility structure predicts social action values only for clergy. The Moral

Majority plausibility structure is inversely related to the fundamentalist plausibility structure and this is undoubtedly due to the opposing stresses that each place on social action. Laity with strong ties to the Moral Majority plausibility structure are not especially susceptible to leadership influence. There is no reason to assume that these Moral Majoritarians are participating in social action activities because they are especially susceptible to leadership influences. But laity with strong ties to cultural fundamentalism are not susceptible to leadership, yet partake significantly in social activism—without the values to warrant them. This is the problem with lay participation in social action endeavors.

Clergy have values more consistent with social action behavior than do the laity. While both laypersons and clergy may engage in social action, only clergy have the social action values to warrant such participation. Because laity lack the social action values which would be consistent with their social action behavior, they are more likely to experience cognitive dissonance as a result of their social action behaviors than clergy. As Stark et al. (1971) have pointed out, the clergy of the more liberal Protestant denominations have presented more politically-oriented sermons throughout the last decade than the more conservative Protestant denominations. It is only in the last decade that conservative Protestant denominations have become politicized. However, Peter Berger has expressed concern over the "effortless linkage between reactionary religion and reactionary politics." It seems that for the New Christian Right the worry is that the Bible may be misappropriated due to a perceived absence of tradition, or historical consciousness that is characteristic among New Right groups (Hill and Owen, 1982). Again, we have the old "it's not *what* 'they' (e.g., the Moral Majority) are doing, but 'how' they are doing it" that is found to be at fault. Carl Henry, one of America's leading evangelical thinkers, claims that the New Right lacks historical perspective, theological depth, and philosophical rationale to be involved politically (*Christianity Today*, March 13, 1981). We discuss the implications of the relationship of fundamentalist social action and lack of fundamentalist social action values in the Moral Majority in the next chapter.

Chapter Seven

Cognitive Dissonance And Plausibility Structures

Leon Festinger and Cognitive Dissonance

Social scientists are quick to note inconsistencies in attitudinal and behavioral patterns. Leon Festinger called situations where there were inconsistencies in attitudes and behaviors "cognitive dissonance." It relates to potential relationships among cognitive elements of any sort and imbalances in those relationships from any source. "Dissonance is a type of relationship that obtains between two cognitions when they appear mutually contradictory to the person who holds or entertains them" (Festinger, 1957:3).

It is often assumed that individuals strive for consistency in their attitudes and actions. If consistency is the rule, then how does the individual handle inconsistencies when they discover them? It should be pointed out that many individuals may not regard differences in cognitive elements as inconsistencies. They simply may never have noticed it. In other cases attempts may be made to rationalize the inconsistencies. But sometimes individuals are not successful in rationalizing the inconsistencies to themselves. When the inconsistency persists, Festinger states that a state of psychological discomfort arises—or cognitive dissonance: 1) the existence of dissonance, being psychologically uncomfortable, will motivate the person to reduce the dissonance and achieve a state of consonance; 2) when dissonance is present, in addition to trying to reduce it, the person will avoid situations and information which would likely increase the dissonance (1957:2,3).

There is no guarantee that the person will be able to reduce or remove the dissonance. However, changes in evaluation will always be in the direction of congruity with the existing frame of reference (Osgood and Tannenbaum, 1955:43).

Festinger defined a cognitive element as any bit of knowledge that an individual might have about himself or the world around him. Opinions, feelings, values and attitudes and knowledge of material objects are all cognitive elements. It does not matter whether these bits of information are objectively accurate, nor does it matter how the individual came to know them.

According to Festinger's theory one of three relationships may apply at a given time between any two cognitive elements: irrelevance, consonance, or dissonance. An irrelevant relationship is one in which neither of the elements in question implies anything about the other. The irrelevance is often situational, and it is always possible that something might happen to bring two previously irrelevant elements into consonance or dissonance. Consonance exists between two elements when they fit together, when one implies or entails the other in some way.

Take the anti-social action stance of fundamentalism. For a true cultural fundamentalist, engagement in social action may produce a state of dissonance because it is not in keeping with fundamentalist values of anti-social action. For new members of the Moral Majority (or those who were new members of the Moral Majority at its inception) we should expect a good deal of cognitive dissonance. For those Moral Majority members who have strong ties to the Moral Majority plausibility structure, social action may not create a state of dissonance because social action is consistent with the values of social action inherent within the Moral Majority plausibility structure. Also, they have had time to be resocialized into a pro-action social framework. The magnitude of the total dissonance will depend on the importance of those relevant elements in a dissonant relationship (Festinger, 1957:17). The strength of the pressures to reduce the dissonance is a function of the magnitude of the dissonance.

Dissonance may be eliminated by changing one of the elements in the dissonant relationship. To eliminate dissonance arising from social activism, a fundamentalist would need to change the element of "anti-social action" value to "pro-social action" value. As we will see, this seemingly simple change is quite difficult to make. While the churches who support the activities and social actions of the Moral Majority succeed in getting laity involved in the performance of social actions, little attention has been paid to helping the lay member establish the necessary *values* of social activism. Perhaps more time is needed (a generation?) to achieve the necessary values to make social action a stable part of the cognitive cluster of acceptable religious actions for the layperson. A reduction in the importance of the anti-social action value would help. While we have evidence that clergy have reduced, if not eliminated, the anti-social action value, we do not have evidence yet that the laity have been successful in this regard.

Taking his cue from Fritz Heider, Festinger holds that consonance should be the natural state between cognitive elements relevant to each other. A dissonant relationship is considered to be disturbing enough to motivate its resolution. Dissonance varies in its intensity and its intensity depends on the importance of the elements (Festinger, 1957:16). In an imbalanced state it is generally assumed that whichever sentiment is strongest will determine which change will occur to restore balance. People will generally make the simpler change.

Dissonance can be reduced by altering one of the cognitive elements, by changing an opinion, reevaluating a chosen or rejected option, or enhancing the importance of a given task. The means used to reduce dissonance may vary with personality, culture and situation, but the motivation to reduce this dissonance is universal.

> The basic background of the theory consists of the notion that the human organism tries to establish internal harmony, consistency, or congruity among his opinions, attitudes, knowledge, and values. That is there is a drive toward consonance among cognitions (Festinger, 1957:260).

Cognitive dissonance reducing mechanisms restore consonance to the cognitive elements or sever the connection between cognitive elements, thus causing them to be irrelevant to one another (so motivation may be involved). Though dissonance can never be totally eliminated, it can be reduced by dissonance-reducing or dissonance-avoiding behavior.

Festinger's cognitive dissonance theory does not specify the strategies for measuring the conditions under which these processes will occur. Research must find the limiting conditions in each case. According to Festinger, participating in a discrepant behavior would itself cause a change in attitudes.

Applied to Moral Majoritarians, after recognizing that behavior being engaged in (i.e., social action) was dissonant with cognitive components such as religious beliefs and theology, the religious beliefs and theology might be modified to allow for consonant relations with social action behavior. For example, to reduce the cognitive dissonance resulting from social action, the belief that "the world is doomed," might be suppressed while the belief that "God will bless the nation who obeys His laws" might be elevated. Elevating one component ("God will bless the nation who obeys His laws") could provide the needed rationale for engaging in social activism aimed at achieving "righteous" behavior. Suppressing the other component ("the world is doomed") would be useful in suppressing the pessimistic and fatalistic view of the world's future that might make social action seem futile. Another cognitive dissonance reducing mechanism might be the addition of rationales that society has become so wicked and the security of the family threatened, that fundamentalist Christians must involve themselves politically to create a safer environment for their own children. By adding a new cognition, i.e., "The world must be made safe for MY children; though the world may be 'going to hell' after all, it can do so after my children are raised!" the relationship between the existing cognitive elements is altered. These cognitive dissonance reducing mechanisms would provide the necessary conditions to modify the church teaching promoting social isolationism to that of upholding pro-social action behaviors. These cognitive dissonance reducing mechanisms do not necessarily emerge from the followers of a social movement. The leaders of a given movement may provide such mechanisms. In the case of the Moral Majority, Falwell and other New Right leaders have provided rationales for their followers via television and intense literature distribution. While reducing doubts and cognitive dissonance, huge masses of followers and money are gleaned for the purposes specified by the leaders.

Since Festinger (et al. 1956) wrote *When Prophesy Fails*, social scientists have often assumed that those who subscribe to unconventional beliefs consistently face the problem of reconciling discrepancies between belief and experience. This is often said to create a state of "cognitive dissonance." Much work has been done in trying to measure cognitive dissonance and identifying various mechanisms for resolving it (Abelson, et al., 1968; Dunford and Kunz, 1973; Festinger, 1957; Prus, 1976). But as Bem (1970) and Snow and Machalak (1982) point out, cognitive dissonance may be less of a problem for the believer than for the researcher.

Doubt has been cast on much of the work regarding cognitive dissonance. As Benassi, et al. (1980) and Snow and Machalak (1982) point out, "...the subjects apparently never experienced dissonance because they simply failed to absorb the fact that these beliefs were being challenged...the pattern was of subjects blindly ignoring input rather than resisting it" (quoted in Snow and Machalak, 1982:23).

> As Snow and Machalak go on to say, "unlike belief in science, many belief systems do not require consistent and frequent confirmatory evidence. Beliefs may withstand the pressure of disconfirming events not because of the effectiveness of dissonance-reducing strategies, but because disconfirming evidence may simply go unacknowledged....They may not keep their antennae up for signals of falsification. And if, in fact, the signals are transmitted, they are by no means necessarily received.

Snow and Machalek caution social scientists not to project their own criteria for belief onto their subjects who may not be scientifically or philosophically bent (1982:23).

In fact, beliefs based on inconsistent reinforcement may be the *most* persistent. The point Snow and Machalak made is not to deny that cognitive dissonance reducing mechanisms are operative in maintaining belief, but that belief is often maintained "because disconfirming evidence, however compelling to the nonbeliever, goes unnoticed by the believer" (p. 23).

Engagement in social action by those enmeshed in the fundamentalist plausibility structure should produce a state of cognitive dissonance predominantly for laity (see Chapters Two and Six). Cognitive dissonance should result because those with strong ties to the fundamentalist plausibility structure do not have the social values that would logically warrant engagement in social activism. Those with strong ties to the Moral Majority plausibility structure ought not experience cognitive dissonance because they should have adopted the Moral Majority's social action values. They have one foot in each plausibility structure: the Moral Majority plausibility structure and the fundamentalist plausibility structure. Any social action they get involved in should be consistent with the cognitive framework which the Moral Majority provides. Since clergy specifically have ties to both plausibility structures, and in fact are often the Moral Majority official for that district or church, we would not expect them to be bothered by their own involvement with the Moral Majority. They have too much invested. The continuing support that Moral Majoritarians receive through their contacts with and influence of the Moral Majority should be functional in alleviating cognitive dissonance for those who otherwise might experience it.

To understand whether Moral Majoritarians are experiencing cognitive dissonance due to engagement in social activism, we asked respondents four questions related to social action. Here is the first question.

1. "Do you see any contradiction between social activism and evangelism?" (See question 102, Appendix D.)

If they answered in the negative, the following question was asked.

1a. "Did you ever see any contradiction between social activism and evangelism?" (See question 102a, Appendix D.)

2. "Sometimes it bothers me to be involved in social and political action activities." (See question 105, Appendix D.)

If they answered in the negative, the following question was asked.

2a. "Can you remember a time when it did bother you to be engaged in social and political action activities?" (See question 105a, Appendix D.)

A person could score from 0 to 2 points on the cognitive dissonance scale.

Table 7.1

CONTRADICTION BETWEEN SOCIAL ACTIVISM AND EVANGELISM

	No	Yes
Clergy	50% (n=23)	50% (n=23)
Laity	46% (n=38)	54% (n=45)

In response to the first question, we can see that clergy and laity are nearly split evenly as to who did and who did not see a contradiction between social activism and evangelism. Festinger maintains that the larger number of people that one knows who already agree with a given opinion which one holds, the less will be the magnitude of dissonance introduced by some other person's expression of disagreement (1957:177). "Since knowing that someone else holds the same opinion is consonant with holding that opinion oneself, the more people who agree with an opinion, the more cognitive elements there are which are consonant with the cognition corresponding to that opinion" (p. 177). If these people were not members of a pro-social action organization, it is likely that higher percentages of fundamentalists would see the contradiction between social activism and evangelism than are evidenced here.

For those who reported not seeing a contradiction between social activism and evangelism, we asked the second question.

"Did you ever see any contradiction between social action and evangelism?"

Following are the results from this question.

Table 7.2

REMEMBRANCE OF CONTRADICTION BETWEEN SOCIAL ACTIVISM AND EVANGELISM

	No	Yes
Clergy	79% (n=15)	21% (n= 4)
Laity	84% (n=27)	16% (n= 5)

For those responding that they do not see a contradiction between social activism and evangelism, 21% clergy and 16% laity at one time did see a contradiction here. This is a total of 48% (n=27) clergy and 60% (n=50) laymembers who at some time saw a contradiction between social action and evangelism.[1] Since this data is dependent on self-reports of a past mental attitude, we do not know how accurate the recall is. It is quite possible that motivation is present to keep one from remembering such a contradiction, or it is possible that the respondent truly does not remember it, or it is possible, as Snow and Machalek (1982) point out, that they never truly saw a contradiction, hence not experiencing dissonance.

The third question relating to cognitive dissonance was (question 105):

"Sometimes it bothers me to be involved in social and political action activities."

The response was as follows:

---

[1] We lost 25% of the clergy and 7% of the laity who either did not know if they saw the contradiction or who could or did not follow the skip pattern of this question correctly.

Table 7.3

BOTHERED TO BE INVOLVED IN SOCIAL ACTION

	No	Yes
Clergy	59%	41%
	(n=27)	(n=19)
Laity	59%	41%
	(n=51)	(n=35)

Clergy and laity percentages of those bothered by engagement in social activism here were identical.

For those who reported not being bothered by involvement in social and political action activities, the follow up question was asked (105a):

"Can you remember a time when it did bother you to be engaged in social and political action activities?"

Table 7.4

REMEMBERED WHEN SOCIAL AND POLITICAL ACTION WAS BOTHERSOME
(Percentage responding "no" in Table 7.3)

	No	Yes
Clergy	75%	25%
	(n=18)	(n= 6)
Laity	83%	17%
	(n=40)	(n= 8)

This results in a total of 54% (n=25) of the clergy and 50% (n=43) of the laymembers responding were that they were aware of being bothered at some time for their engagement in social and political action activities. Thirty-nine percent (n=18) of the clergy and 47% (n=40) of the laymembers reported never being bothered by engagement in social and political action.[2] By the Moral Majority's persuading more and more persons over the years that social actions are good and necessary, dissonance should be reduced, even the memory of it. If all Moral Majoritarians were persuaded of the consistency of their social activism with the Gospel, Scripture, and world necessity, the dissonance would undoubtedly be rendered negligible (cf. Festinger, 1957: 202).

Hypotheses

Hypotheses discussed in this chapter include the following:

7.1   Strength of ties to the fundamentalist plausibility structure is correlated with cognitive dissonance for laity only.

This correlation between ties to the fundamentalist plausibility structure and cognitive dissonance is expected for laity because it is they who hold antisocial action values. While associating with a social action organization (i.e., the Moral Majority) which promotes social action behavior, laypersons tend to hold to a plausibility structure which discourages such action. In fact, laypersons have just the opposite—anti-social action values (see Table 6.5). Also, as we have seen, clergy are better able to hold to two plausibility structures than laity.

7.2   Ties to the Moral Majority plausibility structure are inversely correlated to cognitive dissonance.

The Moral Majority plausibility structure should not be significantly correlated to cognitive dissonance because the Moral Majority encourages and avidly supports social action behavior while providing the necessary rationales and "therapies" to instill social action values and to make said action a viable alternative.

7.3   Social action behavior will be correlated with cognitive dissonance.

---

[2] We lost 7% (n=3) of the clergy and 3% (n=3) of the laity who either did not know if they were bothered by engagement in social action or who could not or did not follow the skip pattern of this question correctly.

Because of the traditional fundamentalist ban on social and political activism, we should expect our scale of social action behavior to be correlated with cognitive dissonance. They should be bothered with their social actions because they have been taught for so many years not to involve themselves with it.

7.4   Social action values are inversely correlated with cognitive dissonance.

One of the requirements for cognitive dissonance is an inconsistency in values and behavior patterns. Festinger expected an imbalance among cognitive elements to result in a state of cognitive dissonance (see Chapter Two). Moral Majoritarians who have adopted social action values should not be expected to have cognitive dissonance because they are expected to have incorporated the values of the Moral Majority into their world outlook, hence letting go or releasing themselves of anti-social action biases which would be contrary to their involvement in the Moral Majority.

7.5   Cognitive dissonance reducing mechanisms are not correlated to cognitive dissonance.

Cognitive dissonance reducing mechanisms should not be related to cognitive dissonance simply because cross-sectional data cannot measure the dissonance itself and the item to resolve dissonance at the same time. It would take a longitudinal study to ascertain the relationship.

Table 7.5

CORRELATIONS OF COGNITIVE DISSONANCE AND PLAUSIBILITY STRUCTURES

	Cognitive Dissonance	
	Clergy	Laity
Fundamentalist Plausibility Structure	-.22	.28**
Moral Majority Plausibility Structure	.06	-.14
Social Action Values	-.32**	-.28**
Social Action Behavior	-.07	-.03

** Probability < .01

Table 7.5 supports hypotheses 7.1. Ties to the fundamentalist plausibility structure are significantly correlated with cognitive dissonance for laity. This dissonance is most likely due to the fact that they belong to a plausibility structure which has anti-social action values and consequently frowns on and discourages social action behavior. It is not merely belonging to an anti-social action plausibility structure that is causing the cognitive dissonance. Rather, it is having ties to an anti-social action plausibility structure while associating with a pro-social action organization (i.e., the Moral Majority) that together brings about a state of dissonance. If fundamentalists limited their involvement to a fundamentalist church or organization which continually discouraged social action, dissonance should not result.

Laity with strong ties to the fundamentalist plausibility structure are in conflict involving two opposing conversational fabrics with regard to social action. Cognitive dissonance should be expected to persist as long as they maintain ties with one plausibility structure (fundamentalist) while associating to some degree with an opposing plausibility structure (Moral Majority). As we saw in Chapter Six, the two plausibility structures are diametrically opposed in regard to social action and this is most probably the basis for cognitive dissonance pervading laity with ties to the fundamentalist plausibility structure. An explanation of why this relationship does not hold for clergy is that clergy of the Moral Majority have ties to both the fundamentalist and Moral Majority plausibility structures and thus ties to the fundamentalist plausibility structure do not affect them as it does the laity. Only when clergy themselves lack social action values would they experience cognitive dissonance.

Hypothesis 7.2 is not supported. Ties to the Moral Majority plausibility structure are not inversely correlated to cognitive dissonance. And the inverse relationship for the laity, though not significant, offers a slight hint for the notion that if a laymember has strong ties to the Moral Majority, he or she is less likely to experience cognitive dissonance. Having friends who are members of the Moral Majority (Greg Dixon states that most members do, see Appendix A), donating time to the Moral Majority, holding an office in the Moral Majority and length of time as a member in the Moral Majority all help to bond a person to the Moral Majority and its world outlook. This support system would also serve to minimize cognitive dissonance resulting from one's previous teachings against social action and political involvement. While one's ties to the Moral Majority plausibility structure are not inversely related to dissonance, at least we see that there is no *positive* relation to dissonance.

Hypothesis 7.3 is not supported. Social action behaviors are not related to cognitive dissonance. It is likely that the necessary legitimations are provided by Moral Majority leadership along with social action endeavors as they arise. It is also quite possible that the individual is not experiencing any cognitive dissonance at all. He or she simply may not have made the connection between a value that once was operative and an action that now is acceptable. As Snow and Machalek (1982) point out, cognitive dissonance may exist in the mind of the researcher so that the respondent has no difficulty at all with what might appear to be a contradiction. But as Fishbein (1966) also points out, perhaps we should be questioning our initial assumption that the behavior in question is a function of the attitude we are working with. When convergent validity is not obtained, Fishbein states that a multi-method approach may be useful.

Hypothesis 7.4, that social action values are inversely correlated with cognitive dissonance, holds for laity as well as clergy. This is one area where clergy and laity behave consistently with each other. As long as Moral Majoritarians have social action values instilled in their cognitive framework, they are less likely to experience cognitive dissonance. The problem with cognitive dissonance arises when values of social action are not present to warrant their association with the Moral Majority and/or social action behavior. That cognitive dissonance results from lack of social action values was foreshadowed in Table 6.5 where laity's social action was positively correlated with ties to the Moral Majority plausibility structure but laity social action values were inversely correlated with ties to the fundamentalist plausibility structure. There appears to be a group of "cultural fundamentalists" in the Moral Majority who don't have social action values at all. These should be the Moral Majoritarians experiencing cognitive dissonance. As can be seen in Table 7.5, actual social action *behavior* is far less of an important factor influencing cognitive dissonance than social action *values*. These findings provide additional evidence that laypersons may be persuaded to follow pastors or Moral Majority leaders into social action without believing wholeheartedly in the cause. Wood's research (1981, 1984) bears this out: liberal ministers could persuade laymembers to support social policies against their individual values by convincing them that these actions were in keeping with the broader, more universal values of the church to which both layperson and minister belonged.

How does this happen? How do ministers persuade parishioners to act against their individual wills? A starting place is with the perception of authority that laypeople have. The fundamentalist model of authority is consistent with Weber's "charismatic" authority type. Viewing fundamentalist leadership in the mold of the Biblical prophets, fundamentalists understand their pastors to speak under divine inspiration and guidance when they speak from the pulpit. As a fundamentalist organization, the Moral Majority has maintained this "charismatic" mode of leadership. Both Jerry Falwell and Greg Dixon readily quote the prophets Jeremiah, Elijah, Nathan, and others when defending their admonitions to society and the government. Sunday after Sunday fundamentalist pastors speak out against sin and moral decay and preach evangelistic messages. Pastors have the full support of their laity. When a fundamentalist pastor has credibility in the eyes of his congregation and begins to "change the tune" of his Sunday sermons, many laypersons may follow him in whatever "new direction" he advocates, as long as the "new direction" takes place gradually, sounds "plausible," and "inspired" like the prophets. Whether preaching the pro-evangelism message of classical fundamentalism or the pro-social action message of modern Moral Majoritarinism, the prophets are referred to for legitimation, inspiration, and activation of the laity. The minister may not be aware that he is "changing his tune," however, from my interviews of Moral Majority leaders who also are pastors, it is clear that they are aware of the transition from anti-social action values to pro-social action values. In fact, most laypersons are aware of this change also. Seventy-five percent of my sample remember when their own churches preached an anti-social action gospel.

The cross-tabulations in Table 7.6 and Table 7.7 provide additional evidence that our cognitive dissonance scale has a moderate relation to social action behavior and social action values.

Table 7.6

COGNITIVE DISSONANCE AND SOCIAL ACTION

		Cognitive Dissonance	
		No	Yes
Social Action	Lo	17% (n=27)	41% (n=66)
	Hi	11% (n=19)	31% (n=50)

Gamma = .01

Table 7.6 demonstrates the lack of association between social action and cognitive dissonance. We get a similar picture when we cross-tabulate social action values with cognitive dissonance.

Table 7.7

COGNITIVE DISSONANCE AND SOCIAL ACTION VALUES

| | | Cognitive Dissonance | |
		No	Yes
Social Action Values	Lo	12% (n=19)	36% (n=59)
	Hi	17% (n=27)	35% (n=57)

Gamma = -.29

Table 7.7 demonstrates a moderate relationship between social action values and cognitive dissonance. There are more respondents experiencing a measure of cognitive dissonance than are not. A similar number of respondents are experiencing a measure of dissonance whether scoring high or low in social action values.

As we saw from Table 7.5, social action *behaviors* do not necessarily cause cognitive dissonance, but *lack* of *social action values* does. It is likely that the necessary legitimations and rationalizations (cognitive dissonance reducing mechanisms) are provided by Moral Majority leadership along with each social action endeavor as it arises, whereas social action values require more time to solidify and to be incorporated into one's cognitive framework. Also, dissonance may not exist or appear until a discrepancy is brought to the individual's attention, in this case by being asked about the contradiction inherent in the fundamentalist worldview and social action behavior (cf. Snow and Machalek, 1982).

In sum, we have a body of Moral Majoritarians who admittedly are experiencing a measure of dissonance due to their anti-social action values. How are these people handling this discrepancy? How are they addressing it so that it doesn't cause them to leave the Moral Majority and/or to cease social action behaviors all together? Why don't they develop social action *values*?

To address the issue of how Moral Majoritarians who experience cognitive dissonance minimize it, let us first look at why these same people think that Christians should be active in social action issues. If they are to have credibility as members of the Moral Majority, they must take part in social action at some level. And while looking at the reasons for Christian involvement in social action, we may get a preview of what cognitive dissonance reducing mechanisms or rationales to expect.

I asked respondents why Christians should become involved in social action (see question 103a, Appendix B). Table 7.8 presents the respondents' rationales for engaging in social action. I selected those who have reported experiencing cognitive dissonance for this table. Clergy and laypersons are collapsed in this table due to the similarity in response pattern.

Table 7.8

WHY GET INVOLVED IN SOCIAL ACTION?

1.	The issues are of moral significance.	35% (n=38)
2.	The United States must be a righteous nation if it wants God's favor.	42% (n=45)
3.	Social activism is part of the Great Commission.	2% (n= 2)
4.	To make the world a better place to live.	3% (n= 3)
5.	The issues relate to personal concerns	4% (n= 4)
6.	Other	14% (n=16)
		100% (n=108)

It is clear that Table 7.8 bears out Jerry Falwell's favorite Biblical dictum:

If my people, which are called by my name, shall humble themselves, and pray, and seek my face, and turn from their wicked ways; then will I hear from heaven, and will forgive their sin, and will heal their land (II Chronicles, 7:14).

"The United States must be a righteous nation if it wants God's favor" is a favored rationale for engaging in social action. The second most favored rationale is that "the issues must be of moral significance for Christians to become involved in social action." Other categories of response are so much less important that these two rationales will suffice as major reasons or conditions for engagement in social action even by those bothered by their own social action involvement. Both of these rationales relate to the "righteousness" and "morality" motif of the Moral Majority.

As we saw in Table 2.1, Moral Majoritarians who don't have social action values nonetheless believe that the United States must be a righteous nation if she wants God's favor—or that the issues must be of moral significance to warrant social action. Here is a potential cognitive dissonance reducing mechanism, or legitimating rationale for why one should take part in social action even though he or she has not adopted the social action value system of the Moral Majority.

Table 7.9

COGNITIVE DISSONANCE AND COGNITIVE DISSONANCE REDUCING MECHANISMS

Cognitive Dissonance	Cognitive Dissonance Reducing Mechanisms
Clergy	-.13
Laity	.09
Social Action	
Clergy	-.03
Laity	.48***

*** Probability < .001

Table 7.9 indicates that cognitive dissonance reducing mechanisms are unrelated to cognitive dissonance for clergy and laity. And this is how it should be. Cognitive dissonance reducing mechanisms should not be related to cognitive dissonance because a cross-sectional study by nature cannot detect cognitive dissonance *and* cognitive dissonance reducing mechanisms. If a person had cognitive dissonance it wouldn't show up alongside the mechanisms that were used to either reduce or eliminate it. This is a basic drawback when using cross-sectional data. There is a time factor involved. At time one, cognitive dissonance is experienced. At time two, it is reduced with "legitimations" or rationales. You can't have past and present at the same time. One could expect clergy not to experience cognitive dissonance because of their ties to both plausibility structures and also because they have social action values (see Chapter Six). But laity do not have social action values and many of them have strong ties to the fundamentalist plausibility structure. This makes one wonder if laity are unaware of their own cognitive dissonance (see Chapter Two) or the social action discrepancythat exists between the two plausibility structures.

While cognitive dissonance reducing mechanisms are not related to social action for clergy, for laity a very strong relationship exists. This may be interpreted to mean that the rationales, or legitimating mechanisms are used to temporarily allow a person without social action values to engage in social action. Legitimating mechanisms could continue to be used to allow the participation in social action until values are developed that would allow social action behaviors to become a permanent part of the cognitive schema of viable behavioral possibilities.

We saw in Chapter Six that lay members engaged in social action yet did not have the necessary social action values to accompany their social action behaviors as did the clergy. We saw in Table 7.5 that not having social action values was the likely cause of cognitive dissonance. Now we see that cognitive dissonance reducing mechanisms are related to the social action behaviors—the very element that is inconsistent with the cognitive framework of laymembers who are bound to the fundamentalist plausibility structure. Thus, it may be reasonable that cognitive dissonance reducing mechanisms are unrelated to cognitive dissonance. Lay members may not be aware that they are involved in a discrepant action to the plausibility structure, or they may be suppressing this knowledge.

What cognitive dissonance reducing mechanisms do Moral Majoritarians draw on? We asked those who reported seeing a contradiction between social action and evangelism at any time in the past how they resolved this conflict.

Table 7.10

HOW DID YOU RESOLVE THIS CONFLICT?

	Clergy	Laity*
Practice social action only when necessary; give evangelism priority.	30% (n= 6)	14% (n= 5)
Conflict is not resolved.	10% (n= 2)	22% (n= 8)
Through Bible study and prayer.	15% (n= 3)	16% (n= 6)
Gospel solves social ills.	15% (n= 3)	14% (n= 5)
Other (miscellaneous).	30% (n= 6)	32% (n=13)

*decimals eliminated account for missing 2%.

Clergy's most common response category in Table 7.10 was that social action should be practiced only when necessary thus giving evangelism priority. Laity's most common response category is that *the conflict had not been resolved at all.*

We asked those who reported that it did bother them at some time to be involved in social and political activities if it bothered them because of the following items. We have combined clergy and laity responses because of their similarity.

Table 7.11

REASONS FOR BEING BOTHERED BY SOCIAL ACTION ACTIVITIES

Christians should concentrate on spreading the Gospel.	90% (n=74)
It is God's plan that the world must worsen until the Anti-Christ comes to rule on Earth.	59% (n=49)
I was taught to keep out of social and political issues.	24% (n=20)

The predominant reason for respondent's being bothered by their involvement in social issues is as we said in Chapter One: the emphasis of fundamentalism is to spread the Gospel. This has always been the primary thrust of the fundamentalist movement. God's plan that the world must worsen until the Anti-Christ comes to rule on Earth has also been a major teaching within fundamentalism though there is evidence that this teaching may be in the process of being suppressed due to the increasing social success of fundamentalists (cf. Marsden, 1980). The majority of respondents have not been explicitly taught to keep out of social and political issues as we had assumed in Chapters One and Two. This response category got the weakest response of any of the categories listed.

Following are other rationales Moral Majoritarians who experience cognitive dissonance use to rationalize involvement with the Moral Majority and/or social action. It should be noted here that the following questions were asked randomly throughout the questionnaire and were not necessarily tied to the earlier questions regarding the contradiction of evangelism and social action and whether they were bothered by social action involvement.

Table 7.12

RATIONALES THAT MAY REDUCE COGNITIVE DISSONANCE

God will bless the nation that serves Him and obeys His laws.	98% (n=113)
Evangelism is more important than social activism.	96% (n=108)
In the last twenty years society has gotten more wicked.	96% (n=109)
There is a danger of becoming too active in social action at the expense of evangelism.	95% (n=106)
If America doesn't turn back to God soon, it may collapse.	95% (n=108)
It is time for conservatives to run society.	82% (n= 90)
Even if the Moral Majority doesn't succeed, we must support it because it is fighting for God's side.	75% (n= 85)

We can make the world a better   59%
place to live through our social   (n= 66)
action efforts.

Ninety-eight percent of the respondents agree with Falwell's dictum that God will bless the nation that serves Him and obeys His laws. The good majority (96%) will hold to the fundamentalist value that evangelism is more important than social activism. Nearly the same amount (95%) believe that there is a danger of becoming too active in social action at the expense of evangelism. This verifies the notion that evangelism is prior to social activism. Ninety-six percent believe that society has gotten more wicked in the last twenty years. The same percentage believe that if America doesn't turn back to God soon, it may collapse. Seventy-five percent feel that even if the Moral Majority doesn't succeed, they must support it because it is fighting for God's side. In a different vein, 82% feel that it is the conservatives' turn to run society. And in comparison, only 59% believe that they can make the world a better place to live through social action efforts. This latter reason for social action involvement is probably more typical of mainline Protestant individuals' reasons for participation in social action.

These are examples of the kinds of rationales and explanations that accompany and help establish the Moral Majority worldview. They are also examples of cognitive dissonance reducing mechanisms that may be used to reduce the dissonance that fundamentalists may experience due to involvement in social action and/or association with the Moral Majority.

Summary

We have seen that Moral Majoritarians who are in actuality cultural fundamentalists—those who lack social action values—tend to experience cognitive dissonance for their social action behaviors and/or association with the Moral Majority. One might ask why they choose to associate with the Moral Majority? They don't have social action values; they are experiencing cognitive dissonance; one would think that the logical thing for them to do would be to cease their involvement with the Moral Majority and quit their social action activities. Do they understand the discrepancy in their values and behavior? When they responded that they were bothered by social action activities, hadn't they realized it before? Had they never seen the contradiction between evangelism and social action inherent in the fundamentalist worldview before?

Respondents experiencing cognitive dissonance believe that moral issues and "making the United States righteous" are good reasons for becoming involved in social action issues. While lacking social action values, these respondents feel that these are compelling reasons to disregard their anti-social action values and become involved in bettering society in the only way they know how.

In time it is likely that these respondents will develop the necessary values that will uphold social action behavior and diminish cognitive dissonance. If these respondents strengthen ties to the Moral Majority—and they may if they continue to associate with it—chances are that their allegiance will gradually shift from the cultural fundamentalist structure to a plausibility structure more consistent with their social activism.

Chapter Eight

New Values For Laity

The Moral Majority has constituents from at least two plausibility structures. On the one hand are those people who are tied to the Moral Majority plausibility structure through associations with friends who are also Moral Majoritarians, devoting time to Moral Majority pursuits, holding Moral Majority offices and length of time in the Moral Majority organization. These kinds of connections serve to continually expose members to the conversational fabric of the Moral Majority. On the other hand are those Moral Majoritarians who are really cultural fundamentalists at heart. They still hold to the anti-social action values of cultural fundamentalism, but are persuaded to engage in social actions of the Moral Majority through rationales and legitimations handed them from the leadership of the Moral Majority or that they themselves have devised.

Berger's concept of plausibility structure holds that views of reality, or what people find credible, depend upon the social support that they receive. If an infrastructure is strong and supportive, then the theoretical constructions grounded in them may be taken for granted with unquestioned certitude. In this sample those with more ties to the Moral Majority are more bonded to that plausibility structure. For them the Moral Majority is a strong and supportive sociopolitical force. These members have adopted the social action value system consistent with the sociopolitical concerns and activities of the Moral Majority organization.

Why are those people who are still bound to the fundamentalist plausibility structure associating with a political organization which supports actions and values that oppose the plausibility structure of these members? The answer seems to correspond with the reason why the Moral Majority has been so successful as the largest New Christian Right political organization: the Independent Baptist church network. Seventy-three percent of our sample attend Independent Baptist churches.

And the great majority of state chairmen also pastor Independent Baptist churches. It seems to be the connection of Moral Majoritarian laypeople with Independent Baptist churches and pastors who serve as the bedrock of the Moral Majority. This may partially explain why it is that laypersons lack social action values yet partake in social action behaviors as well.

How does a new plausibility structure arise in the midst of an existing plausibility structure? Does the erosion of one plausibility structure first take place followed by values or behaviors dissonant to that plausibility structure? Or do dissonant values and behaviors come first thus initiating a new plausibility structure?

As a result of this research I have come to the tentative conclusion that dissonant behaviors come first, thus creating social action values. A new plausibility structure is originally formed which consists of Moral Majority activist leaders. This would include pastors of the Moral Majority. At the same time, ties to the old plausibility structure do not disappear but begin to play a secondary role for these leaders. More specifically, Jerry Falwell and his cohort of Independent Baptist ministers adopted a new set of social values and hence advocated social action to their people. The fundamentalist doctrine (usually premillenial - dispensationalism) is still intact but it has been enlarged to include what once was considered to be discrepant behavior. Their following—largely members of Independent Baptist churches—followed them in their social action endeavors, but without adopting the social action values necessary to sustain an independent interest in social action issues. Social action behaviors without the necessary accompanying values would lead to a state of cognitive dissonance for laity but for clergy (or laity who have social action values), cognitive dissonance doesn't result (see Table 7.5) because their social action is consistent with their social action values.

Why are cognitive dissonance reducing mechanisms related to social action but not cognitive dissonance for laity? It appears that laymembers either (1) are not aware of the social action dilemma that has led to the creation of a new plausibility structure, (2) they were once aware of the problem of social action, but have since rationalized the problem away, or (3) they have learned to justify each social action as it became necessary, thus being unable or refusing to adopt social activism as a permanent part of their role set. In this way, they may never have had to acknowledge the discrepancy between cultural fundamentalism and social action or a change in social action policy.

Besides Festinger's theory of cognitive dissonance there are other structural solutions which may be useful to reduce conflict experienced due to competing role expectations. Merton (1967) addresses the problem involved when people of a given social location experience conflict within their complement of role relationships. When a certain role competes or conflicts with another, structural mechanisms may enhance or even restore stability within one's role set.

Using Moral Majoritarians who have strong ties to the fundamentalist plausibility structure as an example, let's look at what mechanisms might be used to keep one's role as a cultural fundamentalist from conflicting with the additional role of oneself as a socially active Moral Majoritarian, Merton outlines several mechanisms for reducing conflict inherent in conflicting roles. These are just as useful as Festinger's theory of cognitive dissonance in explaining discrepant cognitive elements. Here are some that may especially pertain to the case of cultural fundamentalists engaging in Moral Majority social action pursuits.

1. One mechanism might be to participate differently in each plausibility structure. Two conflicting roles could be maintained with varying degrees of intensity. Perhaps the individual identifies mainly as a traditional fundamentalist Christian and only secondarily as an active Moral Majoritarian. This mechanism is consistent with Festinger's idea of increasing the importance of one cognitive element and decreasing the importance of another to achieve consonance among cognitive elements.

2. Another mechanism for stabilizing one's role set is the social insulation of one or more role activities from observation by members of the role set. For example, fundamentalists may attend church in one setting that is separate and distinct from the social setting where Moral Majority activities take place. Therefore the interaction with each group of the role set is limited and intermittent. Role behavior which is at odds with the expectations of others in the role set proceed without difficulty because everybody involved in the complement of role

relationships is not able to observe the behaviors associated with one's role set. This mechanism would be less a conscious act on the part of the individual and more characteristic of the pattern inherent in the social structure.

I do not believe this particular mechanism is highly applicable to Moral Majoritarians because most church members attend Independent Baptist Churches where the locus of support for Moral Majority activities is apt to take place. It would seemingly be the exceptional case that this mechanism would apply to.

3. Another mechanism for maintaining stability of one's role set is to confront others within the role set with the contradictory demands he or she is making. In the case of the social action dilemma of the fundamentalist and Moral Majority plausibility structures, leaders of each plausibility structure assume that the legitimacy of their demands is indisputable and deserves priority. The layperson's exposing the conflict to leaders serves to redirect the conflict so that it is between leaders of the role set, rather than merely being the layperson's individual problem. The layperson who is torn between one role as a socially active Moral Majoritarian and another as an exclusively spiritually active cultural fundamentalist could be relieved of the responsibility of solving this dilemma by exposing the issue to fundamentalist and Moral Majoritarian leaders. According to this mechanism, it would be incumbent on the leadership of the two plausibility structures to resolve the contradiction. However, in our case, since the representative leaders of both plausibility structures are often one and the same (i.e., pastors who are officials of the Moral Majority), this leader can easily resolve the dilemma through use of rationales, therapies and legitimating mechanisms provided followers, as Festinger's theory of cognitive dissonance asserts (see Chapter Seven). Through the Moral Majority Report and television specials, Falwell has continually addressed this issue for members of the Moral Majority. This mechanism for reducing role conflict has as its condition that the layperson understand the dilemma and is able to articulate the dilemma to leaders. From my interviews with Greg Dixon, Roy McLaughlin, and numerous other Independent Baptist ministers who are Moral Majority leaders, I have determined that they are fully aware of the dilemma their parishioners are in. Dixon maintains that his Moral Majoritarian pastors are often accused of compromising the Gospel. A healthy aspect of this

particular mechanism resides in the fact that the laymember would be fully aware of the discrepancy between the expectations of the two role sets and could confront the leader with it. By demanding the explanation for the contradictory role expectations, the laymember is enabled a more permanent and satisfying resolution that should in turn alter the value system. In the case of laymembers within the Moral Majority, this would be a highly desirable outcome. As it is, not very many laymembers are working on the discrepant cognitions in question.

4. When it is recognized that others in the same social status are also experiencing difficulty in dealing with their role sets, a normative system may develop "which anticipates and thereby mitigates the conflicting demands made of those in this status" (Merton: 378). Social support is obtained and the need is minimized for the individual to improvise private adjustment to the conflict situation. The cognitive fundamentalist who understands the contradiction between the traditional fundamentalist demand to abstain from social action and the Moral Majority mandate to engage in social action may find that there are many other laypersons who are also caught in the same dilemma. The social support they may offer each other would help the individual maintain stability in his role set. In our case this mechanism also assumes that the cultural fundamentalist is aware of the social action dilemma. Otherwise the problem could not be shared with like-minded others.

5. The individual may also make a complete break from those relationships that are causing incompatible demands, leaving a consensus of role expectations among those that remain. This mechanism is consistent with Festinger's theory of cognitive dissonance in that cognitive elements are severed in order to void dissonance. This mechanism also requires that the remaining relationships in one's role set are not substantially damaged by this device. This avenue may be a difficult one to take considering that the role set often involves a network of personal friendships. Dixon maintains that most Moral Majoritarians have numerous friends in the Moral Majority. However, in the case of the Moral Majority, if the cultural fundamentalist did not break with the Moral Majority organization altogether (which if he/she did would be impossible to observe in our cross-sectional study of Moral Majority members), the person might retain his status as a Moral Majoritarian but

cease his or her role in social action activities. This would appear to be highly illogical but I did have one respondent castigate Jerry Falwell for his social activism. This is an odd response from someone who obviously paid her twenty dollars to become a member of the Moral Majority which is billed as a political social action organization, not a religious one.

These mechanisms for articulating roles in one's role set are useful for understanding how the social structure may be modified to keep conflicting demands associating with competing roles from causing disorganization and stress to individuals in a given role set.

Commonalities

What do the Moral Majority and cultural fundamentalists have in common? Since the Moral Majority grew out of traditional fundamentalism, there must still be a lot they have in common. The Moral Majority and cultural fundamentalism have a basic disagreement regarding the value of social action though this may change within the next decade or so. It will take a generation or so for social action values to become socialized into fundamentalist laypersons within the Moral Majority. One thing fundamentalists and the Moral Majority do have in common is their basic concern for a high moral standard and righteousness as a people. When asked if there were a danger in becoming too active in social actions at the expense of evangelism, Dixon responded positively without any hesitation,

> Yes. We must take our responsibility seriously to be good citizens. But good citizenship can never take the place of being a good Christian. Just as Nathan as prophet pointed his finger at David and said 'Thou are the man,' we must warn our people when illegal or immoral politicians and leaders are leading us astray. The Bible provides certain guidance and direction for voting. Other examples in history are Micaiah and Jeremiah who also spoke out politically against what was going on in their times.

This common element may be a key factor in understanding how people change from one plausibility structure to another. While stressing one element that people of a given plausibility structure adhere to, a lesser element is modified. Because attention is concentrated on the more crucial common element, a lesser but still important component is changed allowing for a shift in attitudes. The shift was easily facilitated in the case of the Moral Majority because the change in social action behavior came through fundamentalist churches and ministers who could provide plausible legitimations along with Sunday's "message from God."

Some respondents who at one time were cultural fundamentalists are now located within the Moral Majority plausibility structure as well. They once saw the contradiction between social action and evangelism, or were once bothered by engagement in social action, but no longer are. They have in some way resolved the dilemma over social action, thus adopting social action values. The rationales that might have been once instrumental in reducing dissonance are now part of the therapy and worldview of the Moral Majority. There is always the possibility that these people who now strongly adhere to the Moral Majority plausibility structure never were cultural fundamentalists in the sense that I have explained. However, that explanation is unlikely. The data reveal that the laity are overwhelmingly cultural fundamentalists. I can hardly imagine a pastor of an Independent Baptist church not having been born and bred a cultural fundamentalistas well. Falwell came at a propitious moment in history when many fundamentalists were accepting of a shift toward social action. With the Moral Majority Falwell and others provided the vehicle for expression for many who wanted a taste of social and political action and who were upset at the direction society had been heading.

Because some fundamentalists have strengthened ties to the Moral Majority plausibility structure while weakening those to the fundamentalist plausibility structure, this does not mean that religious priorities have been reversed. Even committed Moral Majoritarians who are avid social activists insist that evangelism still takes priority as the Great Commission. The main difference in the worldviews supported by the two plausibility structures appears to be that the Moral Majority advocates social action to achieve its goals and the fundamentalists have not yet inculcated political action values into their realm of plausible actions. The stress is still on evangelism. One thing seems to be sure, the Moral Majority is not a passing fad. Hadden (1985:25) believes we are viewing the front end of the movement while Pierard (1983) and Neuhaus (1984) believe the Moral Majority has already peaked. Though Hadden is skeptical about the Religious Right's ability to create a "moral America," the movement doesn't fade away when the press turns to another story. Another reason the Moral Majority shouldn't be expected to fade is because they are addressing needs of a wider audience than heretofore has been believed to be the case (Hadden, 1985:25). And, as Rodney Stark has pointed out, the populace *is* with the Moral Majority on the *issues* (Ostling, 1985).

How does the Moral Majority persuade fundamentalists to engage in social action activities? Political organizations expose their members to specifically political stimuli. In this case it is often done every Sunday morning right from the church pulpit. The member is exposed to conversation about politics or politically relevant activities of the organization itself. These political exposures increase members' interest in politics and leads them to a greater participation in political activity (cf. Verba and Nie, 1972:186).

Though all respondents were members of this particular Midwestern chapter of the Moral Majority, we can see that it is not mere membership that causes increased political participation. Strongly integrated members of the fundamentalist plausibility structure are also members of the Moral Majority and maintain strong anti-social action values at the same time. Membership in a political organization like the Moral Majority is a necessary condition for the individuals' exposure to further political stimulation within this organization, but by itself will not cause increased political activities (Verba and Nie, p. 190). Over time, however, values of social and political action may be established.

Some cultural fundamentalists may be slowly moving into the Moral Majority plausibility structure and we may have caught them in transition. Hence, through time these cultural fundamentalists who do not yet hold social action values are likely to adopt them as long as they remain members of the Moral Majority and depending on how long the Moral Majority remains on the political scene. Meanwhile, a substantial proportion of respondents who are still tied to the fundamentalist plausibility structure are able to use legitimating mechanisms to reduce the cognitive dissonance which results from their engagement in a social action organization or in social action itself. Festinger maintains that one cannot remain unaffected by taking part in actions discrepant with one's cognitive framework. Therefore, in time pro-social action values should result by those participating in social action and/or a social action organization. The lack of social action values may be only temporary. As long as Falwell can provide immediate legitimating mechanisms for his social action programs, Moral Majoritarians without the values may participate anyway.

One unique characteristic about cognitive dissonance reducing mechanisms in this context is that these rationales are useful no matter which plausibility structure Moral Majoritarians identify with. If in cultural fundamentalism, these rationales may be used to reduce dissonance arising from social activism, as explained in Chapter Seven. However, if in the Moral Majority plausibility structure, these legitimations serve as teachings or "therapy" to keep the "conversational fabric" viable. When one continually hears through sermons, lectures, or by Falwell on television that we need to be socially active due to the wicked state of society, for example, one's worldview may be continually affirmed and ties to the plausibility structure kept strong. This would support what Snow and Malachek (1982) say when they maintain that some belief systems have the characteristics of contributing to their own perpetuation. The use of these rationales or legitimations keeps the Moral Majoritarian with social action values enmeshed in the Moral Majority plausibility structure and worldview and also facilitates the movement of the cultural fundamentalist plausibility structure to the Moral Majority worldview.

What has all this to say about movement from one plausibility structure to another? How can people be persuaded to act in discordance with their plausibility structures?

The closer the worldview of the new plausibility structure is to the worldview of the current plausibility structure, the easier the transition will be. The more radical the difference between the two worldviews, the more difficult the transfer should be. Because the Moral Majority grew out of fundamentalism and does not diverge in any way from fundamentalist theology, fundamentalists were better able to identify and see the plausibility of the new worldview and proposed set of actions. The only thing Moral Majority leaders advocate that would not follow the implications of premillenial-dispensationalism is social action involvement. A radical Marxist, for example, would have very little hope of gaining a fundamentalist following through a Sunday morning television program.

The expressed worldview and philosophical assumptions would be simply too far afield from fundamentalist beliefs to be considered plausible. But Jerry Falwell can get on television, play the role of fundamentalist preacher, talk about the evils of society and how born-again Christians should use their pocketbook and energy to work for a righteous nation so as to gain God's favor, and he immediately becomes plausible to a huge crowd of middle-class fundamentalists. Because he is powerful, "Godly," and a charismatic figure to many fundamentalists, he has power and legitimacy—charismatic authority, to use Weber's terminology—to command a following. There is no successful tradition for Jerry Falwell to follow. He is the first well-accepted fundamentalist sociopolitical action figure to come on the national scene through the television medium and to set up a well-heeled national social action organization for fundamentalists to identify with. Many fundamentalists welcome the chance to exercise political clout—or at least to identify with someone who can. Fundamentalists feel that they have been the needy and the religious minority to mainstream Protestant religion for far too long. They have made some important social gains and they want not only to protect their gains, as the theory of status politics presents (Weber, 1946; Hofstadter, 1962; Gusfield, 1963; Bell, 1963), but they also want to protect a lifestyle based on moral principles (Neuhaus, 1984; Zurcher et al., 1971; Page and Clelland, 1978).

Though some of the issues which groups like the Moral Majority tend to be engaged in often seem narrow in scope, this is not unique to their tradition. Vietnam, busing, civil rights, gay rights, the Equal Rights Amendment, the Nicaraguan Revolution and others, for example, were moral issues of the Left. Both the Right and the Left need a healthy dose of humility to keep them from throwing stones at each others' glass houses.

The complaints of the right also may be a symbol of a larger complaint (Lorentzen, 1980:228). Lorentzen and Pierard do not accept Gusfield's theory of status politics as an explanation for the New Right. Those who protest the loudest may in actuality be grieving most about the erosion of the way of life as they have known it (Page and Clelland, 1978; Lipset and Raab, 1970). Greg Dixon says he doesn't want to bring America to its knees but merely wants to assure that the freedoms fundamentalists have to preach the Gospel and live the way they see fit are not jeopardized. For example, it is possible that threats to fundamentalist church schools are seen as a much wider threat by fundamentalists. An understanding of fundamentalist doctrine (see Chapter One) reveals that fundamentalists are extremely apprehensive over the gains that the Anti-Christ will make in "the last days." Any infringement on the rights of Christians may be seen in "spiritual warfare" terms. Jerry Falwell views his agenda as a holy war. Social action of the Moral Majority has as its roots religious conviction.

Some scholars think protests of devalued groups are in actuality a striving to enhance their sociopolitical positions (Simpson, 1983:203). This view is based on the assumption that culture and power are separate elements in modern democratic social systems and that the cultural threat which one group may pose for another is distinct from the capacity of a group to impose mores and lifestyle on others through politics. Modernism has always been a threat to fundamentalism but so has the cultural fundamentalism complex posed a threat to the modern temper, though perhaps less so (Simpson: 203). While politics has been an arena for groups on the decline to express their anxieties, it can also serve as a new-found legitimacy, efficacy, and entitlement to the never-ending race for power and influence in American society (Simpson: 203). Yinger and Cutler (1982) have a more provocative assessment pertaining to the "need" for a Moral Majority constituency. Though they do not think that the United States is in danger of being taken over by the Moral Majority or by its political campaigns, they feel that there is a far greater danger that society will not learn to see the cultural illness of which the Moral Majority is a powerful symptom. They ask "If the values of the Moral Majority seem ill-suited to the contemporary world, what do we have to offer to take their place?"

As Neuhaus (1984) points out, the exclusion of particularist religious and moral belief from public discourse—with the resultant "naked public square"—leads toward the state-as-church, toward totalitarianism. Of course, the available form of totalitarianism, an aggressively available form, is Marxist-Leninism. With religion viewed as a repressive imposition, some would cast out the devil of particularist religion and thus put the public square in proper secular order. Having cast out the one devil, they unavoidably invite the entrance of seven devils worse than the first (p. 86).

By looking past the *ad hominems* often directed toward the religious New Right, we edge up to the conclusion that the forces represented by them are here to stay. They will suffer defeat from time to time, but they will not go away as they did in 1925. These Americans "half-marched and half-stumbled" into the public square that mainstream thinkers have felt was their's. They made no apologies for breaking down the door, since they think it should not have been locked in the first place. They show every sign of wanting to take over, for now they are the ones raising questions about the pedigree of their cousins. Representatives of mainline denominations often take pride in their ecumenism. But equally often they refuse to extend this ecumenism to the religious New Right. They may dialogue with gentle Buddhists and ungentle Marxists but to enter into conversation with "Bible-banging pushers of blood-bought salvation and bullishness on capitalism" is simply too much to ask (Neuhaus: 57).

The Moral Majority is not an economic movement; some maintain that its members really would not know what to do with political power if they got hold of it (Simpson, 1983:203). They are frightened by what they consider to be secular humanism creeping over the land and the potential threat this humanism poses to fundamentalists and their families. They are ready and willing to use whatever economic means they have to protect their lifestyle. If Jerry Falwell must raise $100 million per year to keep afloat, his people have certainly been willing to contribute the money. Though his financial needs have increased astronomically along with other New Right "empires," and though he had to lay off ten percent of his staff last year and cut his toll free help line, revenues are still rising. As long as he doesn't misread his following as other New Right leaders have, he feels sure that his people are backing him and that his political agenda is supported by a real majority of the people.

Preservation and protection of lifestyle are often the goals of noneconomic political movements. Lifestyle concern may be the motivating factor of the Moral Majority. The tactics instrumental in achieving these goals may be threatening to forces opposing the movement, but in general, they need not be.

We have seen how mainstream intellectuals were highly upset and threatened by groups of the New Christian Right such as the Moral Majority in the early years of the New Christian Right movement. But those who have closely followed the movement are no longer intimidated. The Moral Majority now is said to have not been as powerful, did not really pose much of a threat in the political arena, and it is debatable whether they really helped Reagan get into the Oval Office (Hadden and Swann, 1981; Kater, 1982). The Moral Majority might disappear into the background just as fundamentalism did after the Scopes Trial and prohibition, but astute observers such as Neuhaus do not think so.

Fundamentalists have not been successful in the past at winning the dominant voice in society in terms of moral behavior. Even when they posed a challenge to moderates and liberals in the early twenties, they failed to win their demands in any of the large mainline denominations (Simpson: 196). Fundamentalists have not been noted for sustained political skill, participation, or even interest. If the New Religious Right and, in particular, the Moral Majority are here to stay, this will be the first political success fundamentalism has had.

Hammond (1983:219) states,

Moral Majority seems unlikely to do more than make headlines and create possible mischief in certain election campaigns." There is really no evidence that conservative moral values will dominate American politics for the rest of this century, yet it is quite possible. Whereas soul-winning served in the nineteenth century as the power behind institution building, its twentieth century expression is seen by some scholars to be merely a divisive, not a unifying, force in a pluralistic world (McLoughlin, 1978:214).

This is the assessment of the Left neoconservative thinker. Neuhaus (1982:52) maintains that "only now is it beginning to occur to mainline religious leadership that the forces that entered the arena under the banners of the religious New Right are part of the new normality."

The fundamentalist plausibility structure seems likely to endure because of its roots in modern society (see Chapter Two). The Moral Majority already appears to have peaked in its force as a social movement organization; it is quite possible that it may fade into history as another movement that came on the horizon for a brief moment, had its moment in the limelight, and passed on into history books as another outcry within cultural fundamentalism for its minority status in society. If it does not totally disappear, the history of social movements indicates that it may become assimilated into American society as another of many organizations that started out as vital movements but ended up as one of numerous organizations trying to keep financially afloat, its name in the yellow pages, and its causes in mainstream thinking.

If the Moral Majority "solution" to America's "broken covenant" is unsatisfactory to Americans, what are the alternatives? Harvey Cox's (1984) scenario for the return of the sacred to the secular city is a liberal church vision of repentance and redemption. Neoconservative Richard John Neuhaus would return God to the "naked public square" as a first step in restoration of the covenant (1984). Catholic atheist Michael Harrington (1983) agonizes about "the politics at God's funeral" and pleads for rational re-creation of something like the creation myth. "If there is a general sense that America needs to mend her way so that she can be healed and once again return to greatness, how that is to be achieved is a matter of deep division" (Hadden, 1985:26).

There seems to be a general concensus that the political-religious movement of the eighties is a response to the liberal social activities of the sixties and seventies (Hadden, 1985; Neuhaus, 1984). There is a corresponding similarity of the New Right movement of the eighties in response to the liberal agenda of the sixties and seventies, and the fundamentalist movement of the twenties in response to the liberalism in the churches during the first two decades of the century. While it is tempting to dismiss the Christian activism of the eighties as a backlash movement by persons who have been left behind and are out of step with the mainstream of American culture, as status politics would have it (Lipset and Raab, 1982; Hofstadter, 1962), sociologists and political analysts are being forced not merely to take New Right organizations seriously, such as the Moral Majority, but the issues that they raise more seriously. They may not set forth a sophisticated philosophical rationale for their positions on issues they tackle. As an evangelical philosopher from Wheaton, Arthur Holmes, suggests, the overwhelming disgruntlement of a great mass of people in America—no matter what religious tradition—points up a serious problem within American society. And if mainstream thinkers can agree with Jerry Falwell that "America's Covenant is broken," and that something needs fixing, it behooves mainliners to see if they can do something to effect the mending. It should be more substantial than pleading for a "rational re-creation of 'something' like the creation myth." Hadden (1985) astutely points out that "the liberal tradition in America does not stand in a strong position to direct us out of this perceived condition to cultural malaise. We stand too close in time to too many liberal programs that were supposed to help solve the very problems that now disturb us so."

Falwell's vision of a repentant America has received a lot of media attention to date. Pat Robertson is running for President. Others in the New Christian Right could move into the national spotlight. One thing is sure, the hypocrisy among liberal denominational thinkers reveals itself in its cry for fundamentalists to exit the sociopolitical arena. Since the Scopes Trial, fundamentalists have been blamed for their political absence. When President Eisenhower presided at the dedication of the National Council of Churches' headquarters in New York, nobody complained. But when President Reagan addresses fundamentalist preachers at the Christian Broadcasters meeting, there are mainline protests against government's captivity to religious fanatics. The situations are not identical but the analogy points up the way in which, depending upon one's alliances, an association can seem either normal or sinister. Only now is it beginning to occur to mainline religious leadership that the forces that entered the arena under the banners of the religious New Right are part of a new normality (Neuhaus, 1984:52).

The failure to see that the issues which activate the religious New Right are often part of a new normality has yet another example. Another counter-movement to the Moral Majority, Norman Lear's People for the American Way, has been fighting the New Christian Right generally, and the Moral Majority specifically, since 1981. But ironically, the editors of *Commonweal*, the liberal Catholic magazine, state correctly that "Norman Lear is to politics pretty much what [Moral Majority leader] Jerry Falwell is to theology. They are both television personalities with a natural capacity for packaging the pieties of their separate worlds." Lear's advertisements "combine tabloid style headlines and a few shocking examples or quotations [that are] much like the technique that the religious right employs against 'secular humanists' or 'atheistic liberals'" (Neuhaus, 1984:51).

Millions of Americans have for a long time felt put upon. Theirs is a powerful resentment against values that they believe have been imposed upon them, and an equally powerful sense of outrage at the suggestion that they are the ones who pose the threat of undemocratically imposing values upon others. As they begin to feel more secure about their place in the new normality, the sense of resentment, and thus of belligerence, may decline (Neuhaus, 1984:52).

The co-optation and possible demise of the religious New Right could be successful if opponents modified their unqualified confrontation with the religious New Right. The Moral Majoritarians, as fundamentalists, thrive on confrontation. Opponents assure their own defeat by challenging the Moral Majoritarians to the confrontational games at which they have achieved mastery. The spirit and tactics of confrontational populism are on their side. Not only the spirit and tactics, but also the numbers. It seems quite possible that the Moral Majority is right in claiming that, on a majority of issues, the majority of Americans agree with the Moral Majority (Neuhaus, 1985:53).

Our response to rightist activism will be more honest, mature, and possibly, effective as we move beyond asceticism of form and style in order to engage their arguments.

The quarrel with politicized fundamentalism is not with the fact that it has broken the rules of the game by "going public with Christian truth claims...our quarrel is not so much over the form of religion's role in society but over the substance of the claims made...our quarrel is primarily theological" (Neuhaus, 1985:19). Neuhaus says that if the right and the Left don't start dialoguing, both will contribute to discrediting the public responsibility of religion.

As far as the claim that the New Right engages in one-issue politics, it should not be forgotten that a few years ago civil rights and then Vietnam were the one-issue politics of liberalism. Members of the U.S. Council of Catholic Bishops have issued controversial treatises calling for a partial nuclear freeze and advocating greater economic equality. The list of Left concerns includes South Africa, the Pinochet government in Chile, American support for anti-communist regimes generally, multinational corporations, military spending, the Equal Rights Amendment, and gay rights. Anyone who deviates from proper opinion on these and other questions is thought to be suspect, if not beyond the pale of moral discourse. What the Left sees as movements of liberation the right views as degeneration. The right claims that the left through law and mass media have been imposing their values on Americans who find those values repugnant. To understand the differences of the right and left requires an honest look at the fact that the "imposition question applies in both directions (Neuhaus, 1985:48-49).

Also, both the left and right use whatever resources are available to then advance their own political agendas. It appears that the same phenomenon that Dean Kelley (1972, 1984) observed in the nonecumenical or conservative sects may apply equally as well to New Right political groups: they are willing to put their money where their mouth is. People for the American Way claims 250,000 members and a budget of $8 million. The Moral Majority claims a membership list of 6.5 million members (thought by many observers to be highly exaggerated) and a budget of over $100 million.

The issue is not one of "using" religion, but of whether one thinks the left or the right is *right*. What one person sees as exploitation to another is exercise of responsibility.

Every tactic the New Right is accused of using in their propaganda is also used by the left. Even Hadden and Swann (1981), who are not known for their support of the New Right, identify an A.C.L.U. newspaper ad in the New York *Times* as "hysterical" (1981:146). This is what the ad said:

> Their (Moral Majority's) agenda is clear and frightening. They mean to capture the power of government and use it to establish a nightmare of religious and political orthodoxy...they are *dangerously deceptive*...the new evangelicals are a radical anti-Bill of Rights movement. They seek not to conserve traditional American values, but to *overthrow* them (emphases mine) (Hadden and Swann, 146).

It has now been realized that there was much overreaction to the Moral Majority's perceived power. The new reaction to a more realistic appraisal of the true influence of the 1980 and 1984 national elections is disgust because now instead of possessing awesome and fearsome power, the Moral Majority is not seen to have that awesome power. The mainline reaction to the Moral Majority seems straightforwardly to be a prejudice over a group of people whose values run counter to the present interests of those in power.

What are we to say of the opposition to the New Right? The People for the American Way has a board of advisors made up of some heavyweight religious leaders such as Father Theodore Hesburgh, president of the University of Notre Dame; M. William Howard, president of the National Council of Churches; Rabbi Marc Tannenbaum of the American Jewish Committee; William P. Thompson, stated cleric of the United Presbyterian Church; Bishop James K. Matthews, former presiding bishop of the United Methodist Church; and Colin Williams, former dean, Yale University School of Divinity.

Considering the impressive array of credentials of those serving on the board, it was considered amazing that in one of the advertisements Lear put on the air, he compared preferences as to how eggs should be cooked—scrambled, poached, fried—with the alleged imposition that the Moral Majority would make on everybody doing things "one way." Lear's point was that in America everybody should be free to do his own thing. In response, Neuhaus has pointed out (1984:50):

> this is a fatuous trivialization of the questions exercising so many Americans. Given his trivialization of religiously based moral concerns, e.g., what forms of meaningful human life are entitled to constitutional protection, over the role of punishment in criminal justice, over parental authority in education, it is extraordinary that Mr. Lear was able to gain the endorsement of some of the country's most prominent religious leaders.

Not all religious leaders are insensitive, however. Monsignore George Higgins, who was early recruited by Norman Lear for the advisory board of People for the American Way, resigned in August 1982 due to the "letter and spirit" of some of the organization's activities (Neuhaus, 1984:51).

Higgins believes that much of the Leftist reaction to the rightist reactionaries reveals "a deep-seated and almost fanatical abhorrence of any and all forms of religious fundamentalism...." Higgins, for one, calls upon liberals to take seriously the religious right's concern about "the breakdown of moral values in American society" (quoted in Neuhaus; 1984:51).

As James Kilpatrick has pointed out, the "sawdust apostle (Jerry Falwell) and his God-fearing flock (Moral Majority) have every right to pursue their political aims in whatever legal way they wish" (quoted in Hadden and Swann: 149). This is their Constitutional right and this is probably the most difficult notion that thinkers with leftist sentiments have to grapple with. They simply don't agree. Hadden and Swann (1981:151) have said that, "what appeared *illegitimate* (emphasis mine) about the New Christian Right's move into politics was the *way* (emphasis not mine) in which it took place." The *way* meant 1) tactics used, 2) being involved without being aware of the issues, 3) what *they* might do to violate the rights of others if *they* gained power, and 4) the application of "Christian principles" in evaluating a candidate as a violation of separation of church and state.

Daniel Maguire (1982:40) also maintains that the issue is not *whether* religion has its legitimate place under the political sun, ...but *how is religion being used*? If you can't knock *what's* being done, the next best thing to attack is *how* it is being done—especially if what is being done is coming from a powerful source that is working against your interests.

Hadden and Swann are correct when they note that, "if there is condemnation in the rhetoric of fundamentalist preachers when they chastise 'modernists' or 'liberals' for not accepting the Bible as the inerrant, literal truth of God, the condescension in the language of the liberals is no less real when they call fundamentalists 'shallow,' assert that they have not 'really' studied the Bible, and therefore imply that they are nobodies" (152).

What is most offensive to conservatives is the liberals' attitude of ontological superiority—the fact that they take for granted the intellectual and moral superiority of their perspective (Hadden and Swann: 153).

Near the 1980 election, leaders from fifteen of America's largest Protestant denominations released a statement condemning the New Christian Right as theologically and politically unsound, and, by implication, unchristian. It was entitled "Christian Theological Observations on the Religious Right Movement," and contained the following:

> There is no place in a Christian manner of political life for
> arrogance, manipulation, subterfuge, or holding others in

contempt....There is no justification in a pluralistic and democratic society for demands for conformity along religious or idealogical lines (Hadden and Swan, p. 153).

On a different note, William F. Buckley, on his "Firing Line," accused Falwell of not being conservative enough, of being too "moderate on some important issues" (Quebedeaux, 1982:158).

Quebedeaux maintains that the Moral Majority operates differently—politically speaking—from its counterparts on the religious Left (such as the National Council of Churches). Both left and right now do what only the left did a few years ago. Both conduct media campaigns about political issues, and in their own ways, evaluate and "rate" the voting records of Senators and members of the House of Representatives—and so advocate *one* party line. Both register votes in population areas where the unregistered would likely vote for the right (or left) candidates. Both use advertising and direct phone call campaigns to make their point. Both have lobbyists and lawyers when the interests of their supporters (as demonstrated by tangible contributions of money) warrant it (Quebedeaux, 1982:159). And both claim to have found the "Christian" position on a host of political prescriptions.

Though the Moral Majority technically is not a religious organization, but a political one, it does desire the rise of "biblical morality" (as it interprets it) in government. Those who question this integration of concerns as a violation of the separation of church and state do not understand that the doctrine of separation of church and state was formulated to keep government out of the life of the churches. It was *not* conceived to prevent church and synagogue from reminding government of the moral and broadly religious principles it often forgets; and it was *not* formulated to outlaw prophecy, either on the Left or Right (Quebedeaux, 1982:159).

Critics of the Moral Majority judge New Rightleaders (e.g., Falwell) of "ripping off a gullible public in pursuit of their own selfish interests and 'posh' lifestyles" (as has been demonstrated lately by some embarrassing examples within fundamentalism). Quebedeaux maintains that such criticism is usually a function of critics' own personal and class interests. If Falwell and the Moral Majority were promoting left of center interests—with the same degree of authority, say as a

Norman Lear—these critics would never designate them as "authoritarian" in their approach. "It is the case that much of the critics' judgment of popular religion is based, very simply, on their own jealousy of its leaders—their financial 'empires,' their mass 'following,' and the technical sophistication of their media offerings and their organizations" (1982:173).

Jerry Falwell is offended when his critics accuse him of self-centeredness in representing the vested interests of the capitalist business class, just as "secular humanists" are offended when their business class critics accuse them of pursuing their own selfish ends (as in their defense of abortion on demand). The fact of the matter is, no matter which side you speak from—the left or the right, the opposition is most often no different from us (173-174).

It is time for both the New Right and the left to stop throwing stones at each other, calling names, and mudslinging. When the left states that in a democracy "all must be welcomed into the political process" (Maguire, 1982:9), they must realize that this includes the fundamentalist, and vice versa.

A critical indication of developing movement maturity and strength is the ability to put aside ideological differences to work together on at least limited objectives with those who have otherwise been adversaries. Through the abortion issue, fundamentalists in the New Right have been able to work with not only other evangelicals, but Catholics, Mormons, and others with similar values. They are finding a broader range of common concerns and, as a result, their organizational alliances are beginning to extend into other areas of cooperation.

Appendix A

Interview With Greg Dixon, Head Of Moral Majority Of Indiana March 10, 1983

1.   Are you by any chance related to Amzi Dixon who was active in the fundamentalist movement in the 1920's?
ANSWER: No.

2.   Are you the head of the Moral Majority in any other state than Indiana?
ANSWER: No.

3.   How many Moral Majority members are there in Indiana?
ANSWER: About 30,000. There are 500 pastors; 50 counties with monthly meetings; 10 congressional districts with a director over each. The county chairmen are over them. There are 47 counties left to organize. I have a board who works with me over it all.

4.   To what do you credit the rise of the Moral Majority at this time in history?
ANSWER: (Here we discussed the history of the liberal conservative argument. Basically Rev. Dixon said that the liberals stole physical churches and people from the Bible-believing literalists. Instead of leaving the churches alone, the liberals remained in the denominations and captured them for modernist beliefs. Orthodoxy was captured for modernism. Dixon said here that he respected the radicals more than he did the liberals because the radicals left the church alone and got out whereas the liberals remained in the church putting new meanings in all of the old doctrines. He quoted from Emerson Fosdick's book to support his thesis. Evidently Fosdick left conservatism, turned liberal and planned how liberals would

take over the conservative churches, instilling new meanings in the doctrines. Dixon considered this "stealing." And the liberals succeeded in this plan. Accordingly, fundamentalists were kicked out of the denominations and had to start from scratch in store-front buildings on second-rate property while trying to hold on to the old truths they held dear. As people began to wake up, they joined these new churches. These new works were based on Biblical Christianity. The reason it has taken so long to gain influence is because it took 50 to 60 years to rebuild churches, seminaries, colleges, orphanages, that had been taken over by the liberals. At the present, a constituency has been built up to fight back. The impression I received was that Dixon felt that fundamentalists never *weren't* active, but are just now powerful in numbers and resources to make their voice heard.)

(Dixon mentioned that there are isolationist fundamentalists and separatist fundamentalists. Independent Baptists are separationists, meaning that they are "in" the world but not "of" the world. So they have more room for social action activities than the branch that will have nothing to do with the world.)

5.   Is there a contradiction between evangelism and social action?
ANSWER: No.

6.   Is there a danger of becoming too concerned and active in social action.
ANSWER: Yes. We must take our responsibility serious to be good citizens. But good citizenship can never take the place of being a good Christian. Just as Nathan as prophet pointed his finger at David and said "Thou art the man," (prophets always preached to the kings in those days), we must warn our people when illegal or immoral politicians and leaders are leading us astray. The Bible provides certain guidance and direction for voting. Other examples in history are Micaiah and Jeremiah who also spoke out politically against what was going on in their times.

7.   Do you think fundamentalism will return to its stance of social non-involvement?
ANSWER: They could, but they shouldn't.

8.   Are most of the social action issues that the Moral Majority is involved in related to the Christian message of morality? What social actions wouldn't the Moral Majority get involved in?

ANSWER: There aren't too many areas unconcerned with morality. The goal of the Moral Majority is not to Christianize America, though it is the goal of Roman Catholicism, but our goal is to preach, evangelize, and maintain liberties under the constitution so that the Gospel may continue to be preached and our liberties maintained. We want to "occupy until Christ returns." I believe the return of Christ is imminent. We must work as if he will come in our lifetime, but plan as if he will not. The Christian must rejoice and weep at the same time. It pains you deeply to see when the nation goes wrong but we rejoice because our redemption draweth nigh.

9.   Do your people want to hear a personal, comforting message from the pulpit or are they interested in hearing abut working for a better society?

ANSWER: My people want the comforting message. They would rather hear the pastor than the prophet.

10.   What is the chief mechanism that the Moral Majority advocates for social change? What are the best methods, what are the most undesirable kinds?

ANSWER: Democratic methods, voting, etc.

11.   What about the idea prevalent in fundamentalist roots (dispensationalism) which maintains that God uses a powerless, righteous remnant and not organized, powerful groups?

ANSWER: (Dixon glossed over this issue—and I did not bring him back to it after a couple of tries—that conservative Christianity has just now gained its constituency back from the liberals. Leaning on the "prophetic model" of authority, he seemed to see God's chosen as powerful and the ones to call the nation Israel back to repentance, along with her kings.)

12.   According to fundamentalist doctrine and worldview, the world must get worse and worse before the end of time, when the Anti-Christ comes to rule on earth. This is considered to be one reason why born-again Christians have hesitated to become involved in social action. The world is doomed anyway. How is social action to be rationalized in light of this? Are we just postponing judgment?
ANSWER: It is our responsibility to do right no matter what happens. The Lord will come anyway whether or not we work. For instance, if I were a member of the Sanhedrin during the time of Christ's crucifixion, I would not have voted for Christ to go to the cross just because this would hasten His plan. I would necessarily have voted against it—knowing all the while that His plan would be done. Judas cannot say in the Day of Judgment that he helped Christ to the cross and thus to fulfill His plan. No, he is guilty no matter what. As Matthew says, "Offenses must come...." We do not hasten the Evil One just because it is in God's plan. The world will get worse anyway—but that doesn't mean I have to help it get worse.

13.   If we work hard enough, what hopes do we have of actually achieving a Christian society?
ANSWER: It is not our aim to achieve a Christian society—merely to insure that our rights to preach the Gospel and maintain our liberties are safe.

14.   How do the churches that Moral Majority members belong to react to the Moral Majority?
ANSWER: They are fine. They give them no static. However, pastors who have taken a stand for the Moral Majority have lost members of congregations and influence within their constituency because of the strong bold stand they have taken.

15. Considering a tradition of non-involvement, does it bother born-again Christians to be active in social concerns in any way?

ANSWER: Well, pastors who are active in the Moral Majority are accused of "compromising" the Gospel. There is no problem among those who are active themselves.

16. Do most people in the Moral Majority have a lot of friends and family members in it?

ANSWER: Yes, of course.

17. Do most Moral Majority members watch other televangelists?

ANSWER: Yes.

18. Do you run across many people who find it necessary to change churches because of their activities with the Moral Majority?

ANSWER: No.

19. What do liberals most dislike about the Moral Majority?

ANSWER: The fact that they may take the power away from them.

20. How integrated into society would you say that most Moral Majority members are?

ANSWER: They are on the periphery.

21. Do you advocate Moral Majority members to get involved in politics, running for office, etc?

ANSWER: They are just now beginning to do so.

Appendix B

Descriptive Statistics

Variable	Mean	Standard Deviation
Strength of Ties to Fundamentalist Plausibility Structure	5.5	.6
Strength of Ties to Moral Majority Plausibility Structure	8.3	3.4
Engagement in Social Action Behaviors	3.9	2.3
Social Action Values	20.5	3.4
Susceptibility to Leadership Scale	11.8	1.5
Income	4.4 ($15,000-19,999)	1.5
Education (respondent)	5.0 (some college)	1.7
Education (fathers)	2.5 (9-11 yrs.)	1.7
Education (grandfathers)	2.4 (9-11 yrs.)	.7
Age	4.1 (31-49 yrs.)	1.0
Sex	1.3 (male)	

Appendix C

Denomination Makeup Of The Indiana Chapter Of The Moral Majority

Denomination	Absolute Frequencies
None	1
Independent Baptist	119
American Baptist	1
Southern Baptist	1
Northern Baptist	1
Bible Churches	1
Church of Christ	1
Christian Pilgrim	1
Methodist (unspecified)	1
Christian Church	2
Wesleyan Methodist	6
Free Methodist	1
Methodist Episcopal	1
New Covenant Fellowship	1
Independent Christian Ministries	2
Presbyterian (unspecified)	1
Friends	2
Church of God Anderson	3
United Pentecostal	1
Nazarene	3
Miscellaneous fundamentalist denominations	12

These findings do not support Jerry Falwell's claim that the Moral Majority is made up not only of fundamentalist Christians, but also Catholics, Jews, and Mormons. Research by other scholars of the New Right, (i.e., Guth, 1983; Shupe & Stacey, 1981) also question this claim.

Appendix D

Moral Majority Survey

INSTRUCTIONS

1. Please do not put your name on the questionnaire as we want to guarantee that every individual's responses are held in strictest confidence.

2. Please answer every question (unless the directions say that a certain question is not for you).

3. When answering questions with a limited number of choices, please choose the answer that comes closest to the right answer for you, even if it does not fit it perfectly. (After you have marked the closest answer, you may write a qualification in the margin if you like.)

4. Most questions can be answered simply by putting a check in the box next to the answer which comes closest to the right answer for you. For example:

    Do you have a job?   1 ☐ yes   2 ☑ no

All numbers under lines in the grey margins (such as $\underset{23}{\_}$ above) are for our use in data processing and should be ignored.

5. When you have finished the questionnaire, please mail it back to us in the enclosed postage-paid envelope. At the same time, please also mail back the post card found with the questionnaire as it is very important that we know that you have responded even though we literally will have no way of knowing which questionnaire is yours.

Thank you very much for your cooperation; we hope you enjoy filling out this questionnaire.

I. RELIGIOUS BACKGROUND AND CHURCH ACTIVITY

First of all, we would like some information about your religious background and church activity.

1. Please print the name of the local church to which you presently belong.

    Name of local church: _____

2. Have you ever been a member of (or attended regularly) a denomination other than your present one?

                                                   1 ☐ yes   2 ☐ no

IF you answered "NO" to question 2 above, please skip to question 4.

3. What denomination was that? (If more than one, list them in order from the most recent to the earliest. Please give full title if you can.)

    a. _____

    b. _____

    c. _____

4. What was your parent's denominational affiliation when you were living at home?

1 ☐ Same as my present denomination

2 ☐ Other (please give full title if you can) _____

5. What was the denominational affiliation of the grandparent who had most influence on your life?

1 ☐ Same as my present denomination

2 ☐ Other (please give full title if you can) _____

6. When you were living at home were your parents interested in social and political issues?

1 ☐ Very interested   2 ☐ Somewhat interested   3 ☐ Not interested   4 ☐ Don't know

7. Were your grandparents interested in social or political issues:

Mother's parents . . . 1 ☐ Very interested   2 ☐ Somewhat interested   3 ☐ Not interested   4 ☐ Don't know

Father's parents . . . 1 ☐ Very interested   2 ☐ Somewhat interested   3 ☐ Not interested   4 ☐ Don't know

8. Do you read Christian literature: 1 ☐ Frequently   2 ☐ Occasionally   3 ☐ Rarely   4 ☐ Never

IF you answered "RARELY" or "NEVER" to question 8 above, please skip to question 9.

8a. What Christian publications do you read most often?

1. _____

2. _____

3. _____

9. How often do you read non-religious publications (not including newspapers)?

1 ☐ Frequently   2 ☐ Occasionally   3 ☐ Rarely   4 ☐ Never

IF you answered "RARELY" or "NEVER" to question 9 above, skip to question 10.

9a. Please name those non-religious publications that you read most often.

1. _____

2. _____

3. _____

II. RELIGIOUS BELIEFS AND PRACTICES

These next questions are about your religious beliefs and worship experiences. How do you feel about each of these statements?

	Completely true 1	Probably true 2	Undecided about truth 3	Probably not true 4	Definitely not true 5
10. Jesus is the Divine Son of God and I have no doubts about it	☐	☐	☐	☐	☐
11. "There is a life beyond death"	☐	☐	☐	☐	☐
12. "The Devil actually exists"	☐	☐	☐	☐	☐
13. "God answers prayer"	☐	☐	☐	☐	☐

	Completely true 1	Probably true 2	Undecided about truth 3	Probably not true 4	Definitely not true 5
14. "Christ resurrected from the dead"	☐	☐	☐	☐	☐
15. "Christ ascended into Heaven"	☐	☐	☐	☐	☐
16. "God created the world and its inhabitants in six 24-hour days"	☐	☐	☐	☐	☐
17. Jesus was born of a Virgin (Mary)	☐	☐	☐	☐	☐

	Strongly agree 1	Agree 2	Undecided 3	Disagree 4	Strongly disagree 5
18. The Second Coming of Christ could happen at any time	☐	☐	☐	☐	☐
19. The state of the world will become so bad that most of the world will welcome the Anti-Christ when he comes to power with "solutions"	☐	☐	☐	☐	☐
20. If we have a problem, we can go to the Bible for the answer	☐	☐	☐	☐	☐
21. The Bible is literally true	☐	☐	☐	☐	☐
22. There is a real Hell	☐	☐	☐	☐	☐
23. An 'Anti-Christ' will rule on Earth some day as the Bible says	☐	☐	☐	☐	☐
24. It is important for Christians to tell others about Christ	☐	☐	☐	☐	☐
25. Ever since the Fall of man, God's people have had to struggle with a sinful nature	☐	☐	☐	☐	☐
26. Miracles actually happen	☐	☐	☐	☐	☐
27. Born-again Christians will be resurrected as the Bible says	☐	☐	☐	☐	☐

III. MORAL AND POLITICAL ISSUES

Here we list actions that some Americans have taken. Please tell us about each action whether you first took that action more than five years ago, less than five years ago, or whether you have never taken that action.

28. Displayed an American flag at my home.

1 ☐ The first time I took this action was MORE than five years ago　　2 ☐ The first time I took this action was LESS than five years ago　　3 ☐ I've never taken this action

29. Taken part in a rally against an immoral activity in my community.

1 ☐ The first time I took this action was MORE than five years ago　　2 ☐ The first time I took this action was LESS than five years ago　　3 ☐ I've never taken this action

30. Written my congressman in support of a larger defense budget.

1 ☐ The first time I took this action was MORE than five years ago　　2 ☐ The first time I took this action was LESS than five years ago　　3 ☐ I've never taken this action

31. Written my congressman on a foreign policy issue.

   1 ☐ The first time I took this action   2 ☐ The first time I took this action   3 ☐ I've never taken this action
      was MORE than five years ago   was LESS than five years ago

32. If your answer to any of the above questions was "less than five years ago", can you tell us briefly why you did these things in recent years but not before?

_____

_____

For each statement below please indicate whether you would approve or disapprove of the action or situation described.

	Strongly approve 1	Approve 2	Undecided 3	Disapprove 4	Strongly disapprove 5
33. Prayer in public schools	☐	☐	☐	☐	☐
34. Extramarital sex	☐	☐	☐	☐	☐
35. Homosexual acts	☐	☐	☐	☐	☐
36. Premarital sex between an engaged couple	☐	☐	☐	☐	☐
37. Male dominated family	☐	☐	☐	☐	☐
38. Busing school children as a means of achieving racial integration	☐	☐	☐	☐	☐
39. Legislation against pornography	☐	☐	☐	☐	☐
40. Equal Rights Amendment	☐	☐	☐	☐	☐
41. Stronger national defense	☐	☐	☐	☐	☐
42. Balanced national budget	☐	☐	☐	☐	☐
43. Teaching creationism in public schools	☐	☐	☐	☐	☐
44. Strategic Arms Reduction Talks (START) with the Soviet Union	☐	☐	☐	☐	☐
45. Nuclear freeze	☐	☐	☐	☐	☐
46. Evolution taught in public schools	☐	☐	☐	☐	☐
47. Teaching both creationism and evolution in public schools	☐	☐	☐	☐	☐
48. Unconditional support for Israel in U.S. Government foreign policy	☐	☐	☐	☐	☐
49. Abortion when the mother's life is endangered	☐	☐	☐	☐	☐
50. Abortion after a woman has been raped	☐	☐	☐	☐	☐

51. Divorce and remarriage when
    no children are involved ....   ☐   ☐   ☐   ☐   ☐

52. Divorce with no remarriage ....   ☐   ☐   ☐   ☐   ☐

53. Artificial means of birth control...............   ☐   ☐   ☐   ☐   ☐

54. Were your grandparents active in social problems?

   Mother's father .... 1 ☐ Very active   2 ☐ Somewhat active   3 ☐ Not active   4 ☐ Don't know

   Father's father .... 1 ☐ Very active   2 ☐ Somewhat active   3 ☐ Not active   4 ☐ Don't know

55. When you were living at home, were your parents active in social problems?

   1 ☐ Very active   2 ☐ Somewhat active   3 ☐ Not active   4 ☐ Don't know

IV. ROLES OF THE CHURCH AND MINISTERS

The following activities are possible ways in which your minister could spend his time. Please look over the list of activities, then answer the questions below.

1. Charity work
2. Teaching
3. Planning worship services
4. Evangelism
5. Administrative work
6. Creating an atmosphere of warmth and friendliness
7. Preparing sermons and preaching
8. Offering comfort to those in sorrow and in need
9. Speaking out against social issues, such as poverty
10. Taking a stand on moral issues such as abortion
11. Involvement in political issues
12. Sponsoring social activities for members of the church
13. Providing spiritual guidance for members of the church

56. Please choose only one of the above and enter that number of the ministerial activity you think your pastor considers most important
    .... _____

57. Please choose only one of the above and enter that number of the ministerial activity you personally consider most important
    .... _____

Here are some things people have said about ministers. Do you agree or disagree? (If your church has more than one minister, you should answer with reference to the senior minister.)

	Strongly agree 1	Agree 2	Undecided 3	Disagree 4	Strongly disagree 5
58. Ministers have a responsibility to speak out as the moral conscience of the nation	☐	☐	☐	☐	☐
59. Ministers should stick to religion and not concern themselves with social, economic and political questions	☐	☐	☐	☐	☐
60. I would support my minister if he were to participate in a picket line or demonstration on behalf of underprivileged people	☐	☐	☐	☐	☐
61. I am happy for my minister to participate actively in social causes	☐	☐	☐	☐	☐
62. I want my minister to feel free to give a sermon on any social or political issue he strongly supports	☐	☐	☐	☐	☐

	Strongly agree 1	Agree 2	Undecided 3	Disagree 4	Strongly disagree 5
63. The church should direct some of its activities toward changing the structure of American society	☐	☐	☐	☐	☐
64. The best way the church can work to solve social problems is through its missionary and charitable works	☐	☐	☐	☐	☐

65. As far as you can remember, did your church ever frown on social and political activism?

1 ☐ Yes   2 ☐ No   3 ☐ Don't know

V. GUIDING VALUES

Below is a list of values. We want you to tell us how important each of these values is to YOU, as a guiding principle in YOUR life. Use a scale from zero to ten. If you think a value is extremely important, you circle the number 10. If you think a value is extremely unimportant, you circle the lowest number, zero. If you think a value is neither extremely important nor extremely unimportant, circle some number between zero and ten — the higher the number, the more important you think it is, the lower the number, the less important.

66. A COMFORTABLE LIFE (a prosperous life) 1   2   3   4   5   6   7   8   9   10

67. BROADMINDED (open-minded) 1   2   3   4   5   6   7   8   9   10

68. EQUALITY (equal opportunity for all) 1   2   3   4   5   6   7   8   9   10

69. FAMILY SECURITY (taking care of loved ones) 1   2   3   4   5   6   7   8   9   10

70. FREEDOM (independence) 1   2   3   4   5   6   7   8   9   10

71. OBEDIENT (dutiful) 1   2   3   4   5   6   7   8   9   10

72. PATRIOTISM (support for your country) 1   2   3   4   5   6   7   8   9   10

73. HELPFUL (working for the welfare of others) 1   2   3   4   5   6   7   8   9   10

74. NATIONAL SECURITY 1   2   3   4   5   6   7   8   9   10

75. PLEASURE (an enjoyable, leisurely life) 1   2   3   4   5   6   7   8   9   10

76. PUBLIC MORALITY (concern for the morals of the nation) ... 1   2   3   4   5   6   7   8   9   10

Now think back to the time before you heard of the Moral Majority. Did you rate any values higher now than you would have then? If so, go back and put a plus (+) in front of any value you now rate higher because of the influence of the Moral Majority. (For example, if you now rate the first value, A COMFORTABLE LIFE, higher because of the influence of the Moral Majority, then put a plus in front of that value.)

VI. MEMBERSHIP IN THE MORAL MAJORITY

Here are some statements about how people might feel about their membership in the Moral Majority. Do you agree or disagree?

	Strongly agree 1	Agree 2	Undecided 3	Disagree 4	Strongly disagree 5
77. I feel a sense of pride in being a member of the Moral Majority	☐	☐	☐	☐	☐

	Strongly agree 1	Agree 2	Undecided 3	Disagree 4	Strongly disagree 5
78. The leaders of the Moral Majority have the answers I want and I am grateful for those answers	☐	☐	☐	☐	☐
79. As a member of the Moral Majority, I must sometimes go along with decisions I don't like to achieve the goals of the Moral Majority	☐	☐	☐	☐	☐
80. I have more respect for myself since joining the Moral Majority	☐	☐	☐	☐	☐
81. The Moral Majority's leaders help me clarify my values so that I can see that their decisions are right	☐	☐	☐	☐	☐
82. The Moral Majority has an important influence on my attitudes toward social issues	☐	☐	☐	☐	☐
83. On the whole I am more satisfied with myself since joining the Moral Majority	☐	☐	☐	☐	☐

84. The one thing that I like most about the Moral Majority is: _____

_____

85. The one thing that bothers me most about the Moral Majority is: _____

	Strongly agree 1	Agree 2	Undecided 3	Disagree 4	Strongly disagree 5
86. The Moral Majority's leaders motivate me to think things through and come out with the best answers whether or not I agree with them	☐	☐	☐	☐	☐
87. The Moral Majority's leaders give me the information I need to reach my own conclusions . . .	☐	☐	☐	☐	☐
88. Membership in the Moral Majority gives me a chance to associate with people like myself	☐	☐	☐	☐	☐
89. Even when I disagree, I feel a moral obligation to support the social policies of the Moral Majority	☐	☐	☐	☐	☐
90. Membership in the Moral Majority has given me something to be proud of	☐	☐	☐	☐	☐
91. I am always happy to tell people that I am a member of the Moral Majority	☐	☐	☐	☐	☐
92. Membership in the Moral Majority has made me feel more worthy	☐	☐	☐	☐	☐
93. I take a more positive attitude toward myself since joining the Moral Majority	☐	☐	☐	☐	☐

	Strongly agree 1	Agree 2	Undecided 3	Disagree 4	Strongly disagree 5
94. It is important to engage in social activism	☐	☐	☐	☐	☐
95. Since joining the Moral Majority, I never feel useless	☐	☐	☐	☐	☐
96. There are some circumstances under which Christians should NOT become involved in social action	☐	☐	☐	☐	☐

96a. What might these circumstances be? _____

_____

97. How long have you been a member of the Moral Majority?

   1 ☐ Less than a year   2 ☐ One to two years   3 ☐ Three to four years   4 ☐ Five or more years

97a. Which of the following describes your position in the Moral Majority?

   1 ☐ lay member   2 ☐ clergy member   3 ☐ county chairman   4 ☐ district chairman   5 ☐ board of directors

	Strongly agree 1	Agree 2	Undecided 3	Disagree 4	Strongly disagree 5
98. I was interested in social and political problems even before I heard of the Moral Majority	☐	☐	☐	☐	☐
99. I was active in social issues even before I heard of the Moral Majority	☐	☐	☐	☐	☐
100. Evangelism is more important than social activism	☐	☐	☐	☐	☐
101. There is a danger of becoming too active in social action at the expense of evangelism	☐	☐	☐	☐	☐

102. Do you see any contradiction between social activism and evangelism? ....   1 ☐ Yes   2 ☐ No

If you answered "Yes" to question 102 above, please skip to question 102b.

102a. Did you ever see any contradiction between social activism and evangelism? ....   1 ☐ Yes   2 ☐ No

If you answered "No" to question 102a, please skip to question 103.

102b. How did you resolve this conflict? _____

_____

103. There are certain circumstances under which Christians SHOULD become involved in social action ....   1 ☐ Yes   2 ☐ No

IF you answered "No" to question 103 above, please skip to question 104.

103a. What is the main reason Christians should become involved in social action? (Please check only one.)

   1 ☐ The issues are of moral significance
   2 ☐ The United States must be a righteous nation if it wants God's favor
   3 ☐ Social Activism is part of the Great Commission
   4 ☐ To make the world a better place to live
   5 ☐ The issues relate to personal concerns
   6 ☐ Our church leaders determine the social concerns we become involved with
   7 ☐ The Moral Majority leaders determine what social issues we become involved with

   8 ☐ Other (please specify) _____

104. How many of your closest friends are active in the Moral Majority?

    1 ☐ None   2 ☐ One   3 ☐ Two   4 ☐ Three   5 ☐ Four   6 ☐ Five or more

105. Sometimes it bothers me to be involved in social and political action activities ....   1 ☐ Yes   2 ☐ No

IF you answered "Yes" to question 105 above, please skip to question 105b.

105a. Can you remember a time when it did bother you
to be engaged in social and political action activities? ....   1 ☐ Yes   2 ☐ No

IF you answered "No" to question 105a, please skip to question 106.

It sometimes bothers (or bothered) me to engage in social and political action because...	Strongly agree 1	Agree 2	Undecided 3	Disagree 4	Strongly disagree 5
105b. It is God's plan that the world must worsen until the Anti-Christ comes to rule on Earth	☐	☐	☐	☐	☐
105c. I was taught to keep out of social and political issues	☐	☐	☐	☐	☐
105d. Christians should concentrate on spreading the Gospel	☐	☐	☐	☐	☐

105e. Other (please specify) _____

	Strongly agree 1	Agree 2	Undecided 3	Disagree 4	Strongly disagree 5
106. We can make the world a better place to live through our social action efforts	☐	☐	☐	☐	☐
107. Jesus Christ is our model of social activist	☐	☐	☐	☐	☐
108. There is no contradiction between the Gospel and what Jerry Falwell, and other Moral Majority leaders are trying to do..............	☐	☐	☐	☐	☐
109. Secular humanism is opposed to the Gospel	☐	☐	☐	☐	☐

110. How many of the television evangelists do you regularly view?

    1 ☐ None   2 ☐ One   3 ☐ Two   4 ☐ Three   5 ☐ Four   6 ☐ Five   7 ☐ Six or more

IF you answered "None" to question 110 above, please skip to question 111.

110a. Please name the TV evangelists you watch most often.

    1. _____

    2. _____

    3. _____

111. How often do you attend Moral Majority meetings?

    1 ☐ Whenever they are held   2 ☐ As often as I can   3 ☐ Never   4 ☐ We don't have meetings

112. About how much money did you give to the Moral Majority in the past year?

    1 ☐ None   4 ☐ $20 - 39   6 ☐ $75 - 99   8 ☐ $500 - 1000
    2 ☐ Less than $10   5 ☐ $40 - 74   7 ☐ $100 - 499   9 ☐ More than $1,000
    3 ☐ $10 - 19

113. About how many hours do you devote to the Moral Majority in an average month?   1 ☐ Less than an hour

    2 ☐ One hour   3 ☐ Two hours   4 ☐ Three hours   5 ☐ Four hours   6 ☐ Five hours   7 ☐ More than five hours

114. Do you hold or have you recently held any office in your local Moral Majority? . . . . 1 ☐ Yes   2 ☐ No

115. If you felt that your activities with the Moral Majority were getting in the way of your church activities, would you cease involvement in the Moral Majority? . . . . 1 ☐ Yes   2 ☐ No

116. Do you believe that the Moral Majority can turn America back to God? . . . . 1 ☐ Yes   2 ☐ No

	Strongly agree 1	Agree 2	Undecided 3	Disagree 4	Strongly disagree 5
117. I am proud of Jerry Falwell and other television evangelists when I see them on television	☐	☐	☐	☐	☐
118. Even if the Moral Majority doesn't succeed, we must support it because it is fighting for God's side	☐	☐	☐	☐	☐
119. It is time for conservatives to run society	☐	☐	☐	☐	☐
120. There is a danger in receiving too much education	☐	☐	☐	☐	☐
121. Government should not regulate businesses	☐	☐	☐	☐	☐
122. The present attack on private schools is an attack by Satan	☐	☐	☐	☐	☐
123. As long as we pray, God will hear us and save America	☐	☐	☐	☐	☐
124. The news media typically takes the side of liberals	☐	☐	☐	☐	☐
125. In the last twenty years society has gotten more wicked	☐	☐	☐	☐	☐
126. If America doesn't turn back to God soon, it may collapse	☐	☐	☐	☐	☐

127. What is the main thing wrong with society today? _____

_____

128. Jimmy Carter was a good president.

   1 ☐ Strongly agree   2 ☐ Agree   3 ☐ Undecided   4 ☐ Disagree   5 ☐ Strongly disagree

129. What do you think it is about the Moral Majority that liberal members of society most dislike? _____

_____

130. Since you have become active in the Moral Majority, what beliefs have become more important to you?

_____

131. What is basically wrong with liberals? _____

_____

132. What beliefs have become less important to you since becoming a member of the Moral Majority?

_____

133. How do you feel about your relationship to society?

   1 ☐ Thoroughly integrated   2 ☐ Somewhat integrated   3 ☐ On the fringe of society   4 ☐ Alienated

134. Christians should take an interest in drunken driving legislation and ensure its passage.

   1 ☐ Strongly agree   2 ☐ Agree   3 ☐ Undecided   4 ☐ Disagree   5 ☐ Strongly disagree

135. Christian parents should take an active role in seeing that appropriate textbooks are adopted for use in public schools.

   1 ☐ Strongly agree   2 ☐ Agree   3 ☐ Undecided   4 ☐ Disagree   5 ☐ Strongly disagree

136. Should parents become involved in a move to fire their child's teacher if the teacher is a homosexual? . . . .   1 ☐ Yes   2 ☐ No

137. Have you ever given money to support a political candidate? . . . .   1 ☐ Yes   2 ☐ No

138. Have you ever donated money to a political organization that was not related to religion? . . . .   1 ☐ Yes   2 ☐ No

139. Have you ever taken part in a strike? . . . .   1 ☐ Yes   2 ☐ No

140. Have you ever made a telephone call to protest a certain social action? . . . .   1 ☐ Yes   2 ☐ No

141. Have you ever been in a picket line? . . . .   1 ☐ Yes   2 ☐ No

142. I would support legislation making it necessary for future office holders to take an oath of belief in God . . . .   1 ☐ Yes   2 ☐ No

	Strongly agree 1	Agree 2	Undecided 3	Disagree 4	Strongly disagree 5
143. Compromise is necessary in the world to get ahead	☐	☐	☐	☐	☐
144. Religion and politics do not mix	☐	☐	☐	☐	☐
145. This world belongs to the kingdom of Satan	☐	☐	☐	☐	☐
146. Any change brought about in society should come directly from God	☐	☐	☐	☐	☐
147. The state of society and the world must become worse and worse for the Anti-Christ to come to rule and God's plan to be fulfilled	☐	☐	☐	☐	☐

IF you were undecided, disagreed or strongly disagreed with the above question, please skip to question 148.

	Strongly agree 1	Agree 2	Undecided 3	Disagree 4	Strongly disagree 5
147a. Because everything must get worse until the end, there is little reason to take action to ameliorate or alleviate social ills	☐	☐	☐	☐	☐
148. Public schools should be racially integrated	☐	☐	☐	☐	☐
149. The Civil Rights movement was and is necessary for Blacks to receive equal treatment	☐	☐	☐	☐	☐

Here is a series of statements on current affairs and public issues with which some people agree and some disagree. Please indicate how you feel about each of these statements. (Check the box under the response which comes closest to how you feel.)

	Strongly agree 1	Agree 2	Undecided 3	Disagree 4	Strongly disagree 5
150. Labor unions do this country more harm than good	☐	☐	☐	☐	☐
151. Every American ought to take a bold stand in protecting freedom of speech even for Communists	☐	☐	☐	☐	☐
152. Disobeying an order is one thing you can't excuse	☐	☐	☐	☐	☐
153. Big corporations do this country more harm than good	☐	☐	☐	☐	☐
154. The U.S. Government should use the military if necessary to protect investments in underdeveloped countries	☐	☐	☐	☐	☐
155. In American society, any individual with ability and ambition can earn a good income	☐	☐	☐	☐	☐
156. Women, if they work at all, should take feminine positions such as nursing, secretarial work, or child care	☐	☐	☐	☐	☐
157. I sometimes question authority	☐	☐	☐	☐	☐
158. In the long run it is better for our country if young people are allowed a great deal of personal freedom and are not strictly disciplined	☐	☐	☐	☐	☐
159. No crime is serious enough to justify the death penalty	☐	☐	☐	☐	☐
160. When I (if I were to) question authority, I feel (would feel) guilty	☐	☐	☐	☐	☐
161. It is the duty of a citizen to support his country, right or wrong	☐	☐	☐	☐	☐
162. Obedience and respect for authority are the most important virtues children should learn	☐	☐	☐	☐	☐
163. A woman finds it difficult to be happy in life unless she marries and raises a family	☐	☐	☐	☐	☐
164. God will bless the nation that serves Him and obeys His laws	☐	☐	☐	☐	☐
165. There is nothing wrong in paying women less than men for doing similar work when they are not the major "breadwinners" in the family	☐	☐	☐	☐	☐
166. It is the duty of a citizen to criticize or censure his country whenever he (or she) considers it to be wrong	☐	☐	☐	☐	☐
167. One of the most important things children should learn is when to disobey authorities	☐	☐	☐	☐	☐
168. A few strong leaders could make this country better than all the laws and talk	☐	☐	☐	☐	☐

In this section we are interested in your participation in organizations other than the Moral Majority.

169. Please look at the examples of various types of organizations below, then tell how many organizations of each type you participate in. (Enter in the space in front of each type the number of organizations of that type you participate in. If you belong to no organization of a particular type, enter a 0. If you belong to no organizations at all, go to question 197.)

____ VETERANS, MILITARY AND PATRIOTIC ORGANIZATIONS such as the American Legion, VFW, Disabled Veterans, D.A.R., AMVETS, etc.

____ ORGANIZATIONS RELATING TO HEALTH (EXCEPT SICK BENEFIT ASSOCIATIONS) such as Hospital board, Red Cross, American Cancer Society, March of Dimes, County Medical Society, Handicap Club, Registered Nurses Foundation, Nurses' Aid Club, etc.

____ CIVIC OR SERVICE ORGANIZATIONS such as Lions, Kiwanis, Rotary, Chamber of Commerce, Community Chest, Junior League, Boy Scouts, School Board member, PTA, etc.

____ "CONSERVATIVE" POLITICAL OR PRESSURE GROUPS such as Republican party organizations, Conservative Caucus, American Conservative Union, Roundtable, Young Republicans, etc.

____ "LIBERAL" POLITICAL OR PRESSURE GROUPS such as Democratic party organizations, The American Civil Liberties Union, Americans for Democratic Action, etc.

____ LODGES, FRATERNAL SECRET SOCIETIES and MUTUAL (SICK) BENEFIT ASSOCIATIONS such as Masons, Elks, Moose, Shrine, Sons of Italy, Knights of Pythias, etc.

____ CHURCH, RELIGIOUS ORGANIZATIONS such as the American Bible Society, local church, Women's Home and Foreign Mission, Men's Clubs at Church, etc.

____ "CONSERVATIVE" ECONOMIC, OCCUPATIONAL OR PROFESSIONAL ORGANIZATIONS such as Farm Bureau, American Medical Association, etc.

____ "LIBERAL" ECONOMIC, OCCUPATIONAL OR PROFESSIONAL ORGANIZATIONS such as The American Federation of Teachers, AFL-CIO, etc.

____ CULTURAL, EDUCATIONAL, COLLEGE ALUMNI such as Museum Board, Lecture Club, Literary Club, Symphony Orchestra Board, Association for Family Living, etc.

____ SOCIAL, SPORTS, HOBBY, OR RECREATIONAL ORGANIZATIONS such as Country Club, Bridge Club, Camera Club, Flower Club, Boating League, Homemakers Club, etc.

Now we want to ask you some questions about the one organization (other than the Moral Majority) which you feel is of the greatest importance to you personally.

170. Please write the full name of the organization which is most important to you personally _____

_____

171. In an average month how much time do you devote to this organization?

1 ☐ Less than an hour   2 ☐ 1 or 2 hours   3 ☐ 3 or 4 hours   4 ☐ 5 hours or more

172. For how many years have you been active in this organization?

1 ☐ Less than a year   2 ☐ 1 or 2 years   3 ☐ 3 or 4 years   4 ☐ 5 years or more

173. Have you ever held an office in this organization? . . . .   1 ☐ Yes   2 ☐ No

IF you answered "No" to the above question, please skip to question 175.

174. What is the highest office you have ever held?   1 ☐ President   2 ☐ Vice President
      3 ☐ Secretary or treasurer   4 ☐ Committee chairman   5 ☐ Committee member   6 ☐ Other

175. Do you think it's right for this organization to take action
     on political and social issues? . . . .   1 ☐ Yes   2 ☐ No   3 ☐ Sometimes

176. Has this organization ever taken a public stand on controversial and social action issues?   1 ☐ Yes   2 ☐ No

IF you answered "No" to the above question, please skip to question 178.

177. Has it done this . . . .   1 ☐ Once   2 ☐ Occasionally   3 ☐ Frequently

177a. What is the most controversial issue that the organization has most recently taken a stand on?

_____

178. Which political party do you prefer?

    1 ☐ Republican   2 ☐ Democrat   3 ☐ Independent   4 ☐ Other   5 ☐ No preference

179. If a group of people in this country strongly feels that they are being treated unfairly, what kinds of actions do you think they should take in trying to change the situation? Listed below are different kinds of actions that dissatisfied groups sometimes take. After each action, please indicate whether or not you think dissatisfied groups should do this.

  a. Take action such as either boycotting or getting up a petition . . . .   1 ☐ Yes   2 ☐ No

  b. Hold public speeches and rallies . . . .   1 ☐ Yes   2 ☐ No

  c. Stage mass demonstrations with large crowds of people . . . .   1 ☐ Yes   2 ☐ No

  d. Engage in civil disobedience by breaking laws which are considered unjust . . . .   1 ☐ Yes   2 ☐ No

  e. Take actions such as "sit-ins" or "walk-outs" . . . .   1 ☐ Yes   2 ☐ No

  f. March quietly and peacefully through town . . . .   1 ☐ Yes   2 ☐ No

Now we want to ask you some questions about how you feel about yourself.

	Strongly agree 1	Agree 2	Undecided 3	Disagree 4	Strongly disagree 5
180. I feel good about myself	☐	☐	☐	☐	☐
181. I feel that I am a person of worth	☐	☐	☐	☐	☐
182. I feel I do not have much to be proud of	☐	☐	☐	☐	☐
183. I take a positive attitude toward myself	☐	☐	☐	☐	☐
184. On the whole, I am satisfied with myself	☐	☐	☐	☐	☐
185. I wish I could have more respect for myself	☐	☐	☐	☐	☐
186. I certainly feel useless at times	☐	☐	☐	☐	☐
187. I feel better about myself now than I did five years ago	☐	☐	☐	☐	☐

VII. BACKGROUND QUESTIONS

This final brief section asks some questions about your personal background.

188. How old were you on your last birthday?   1 ☐ 17 years or younger   2 ☐ 18-24 years

    3 ☐ 25-30 years   4 ☐ 31-49 years   5 ☐ 50-65 years   6 ☐ 66-75 years   7 ☐ 76 or older

189. Are you .... 1 ☐ Male   2 ☐ Female

190. Are you .... 1 ☐ White   2 ☐ Black   3 ☐ Other (please specify) _____

191. Which income group (below) includes your total family income before taxes in 1982 considering all sources such as wages, rents, profits, and interests?

    1 ☐ $0 - $5,999   3 ☐ $10,000 - $14,999   5 ☐ $20,000 - $29,999   7 ☐ $40,000 - $49,999
    2 ☐ $6,000 - $9,999   4 ☐ $15,000 - $19,999   6 ☐ $30,000 - $39,999   8 ☐ $50,000 and over

192. Using the job categories printed below, please enter the number following the one job category which comes closest to the type of job the following persons in your family hold (or held before retirement or death).

    a. CURRENT HEAD OF HOUSEHOLD .... _____

    b. SPOUSE (But if your spouse is the current head of your household, print the number 88 here ...... _____

    c. FATHER (But if your father is the current head of your household, print the number 88 here) ..... _____

    d. YOURSELF (But if you are the current head of your household, please print the number 88 here) .. _____

    e. GRANDFATHER (Father's father) .... _____

    f. GRANDFATHER (Mother's father) .... _____

BUSINESS AND GOVERNMENT
a. Owners, managers, and administrators — such as the owner of a business, building contractor, office manager, sales manager, banker, school administrator, military officer, etc. 01
b. Clerical — such as bank teller, bookkeeper, secretary, typist, office machine operator, cashier, mail carrier, etc. 02
c. Sales, such as salesman, salesclerk, etc. 03

FACTORY AND NONINDUSTRIAL WORKERS
a. Technician — such as medical or dental technician, computer programmer, draftsman, etc. 04
b. Craftsman — such as machinist, toolmaker, diemaker, electrician, plumber, carpenter, brickmason, welder, etc. 05
c. Operative — such as machine operator in a factory, assembler, truck driver, automobile mechanic, etc. 06
d. Laborer — such as car washer, carpenter's helper, sanitary worker, janitor, construction laborer, etc. 07

PROFESSIONAL
a. Professional I — such as medical doctor, dentist, lawyer, judge, architect, scientist, college professor, etc...... 08
b. Professional II — such as engineer, accountant, teacher, librarian, registered nurse, social worker, clergyman, etc. 09

SERVICE
a. Personal Service — such as barber, beautician, practical nurse, waiter, etc. 10
b. Domestic Service — such as maid, cook, etc. 11
c. Protective Service — such as policeman, detective, guard, sheriff, fireman, etc........................... 12

FARMER, FARM MANAGER 13

HOMEMAKER OR HOUSEWIFE 14

STUDENT 15

193. How many years of school did you complete?

    1 ☐ 0 - 8 years
    2 ☐ 9 - 11 years
    3 ☐ 12 (high school graduate)
    4 ☐ 12 + business or technical school after high school

    5 ☐ 13 - 15 some college
    6 ☐ 16 (college graduate)
    7 ☐ 17 or more (grad work after college degree)

194. How many years of school has your father completed?

    1 ☐ 0 - 8 years
    2 ☐ 9 - 11 years
    3 ☐ 12 (high school graduate)
    4 ☐ 12 + business or technical school after high school

    5 ☐ 13 - 15 some college
    6 ☐ 16 (college graduate)
    7 ☐ 17 or more (grad work after college degree)

195. How many years of school did (does) your father's father have?

    0 - 8 years .... 1 ☐
    9 - 11 years .... 2 ☐
    12 (high school graduate) .... 3 ☐
    12 + business or technical school after high school .... 4 ☐
    13 - 15 some college .... 5 ☐
    16 (college graduate) .... 6 ☐
    17 or more (grad work after college degree) .... 7 ☐
    Don't know .... 8 ☐

196. Are you presently ... 1 ☐ Never married   2 ☐ Married   3 ☐ Widowed   4 ☐ Divorced   5 ☐ Separated

197. How many children do you have?   0 ☐ None (I am not married)   1 ☐ None (I am or was married)

    2 ☐ One   3 ☐ Two   4 ☐ Three   5 ☐ Four   6 ☐ Five or more

198. Do you live in ....   1 ☐ Indiana   2 ☐ Arkansas   3 ☐ Other

The last two questions are asked on behalf of the Moral Majority.

200. What is your evaluation of Moral Majority leadership in your state?

    1 ☐ They do a good job and I am pleased with the leadership
    2 ☐ They do a satisfactory job
    3 ☐ I am less than satisfied

201. How do you feel about financial appeals from the leadership of the Moral Majority in your state?

    1 ☐ Contributions are important to the success of the Moral Majority. I don't mind at all.
    2 ☐ Financial appeals may be necessary, but I wish there were some other way to support the Moral Majority.
    3 ☐ To be honest, I wish the state leadership would not appeal to me for financial support.

Thank you very much for completing the questionnaire. We sincerely appreciate your help. Please remember to mail the post card (enclosed with the questionnaire) as well as the questionnaire. (No message is necessary on the post card; its number will tell us you have responded without letting us know which questionnaire was yours.)

This space has been left for any comments you would like to make.

References

Abelson, Robert P. (ed)
1968 *Theories of Cognitive Consistency: A Sourcebook.* Rand McNally.

Bainbridge, William S. and Rodney Stark
1980 "Scientology: To Be Perfectly Clear." *Sociological Analysis* 41:128-136.

Bell, Daniel
1963 *The Radical Right.* Garden City, N.Y.: Doubleday & Company, Inc.

Bellah, Robert N.
1975 *The Broken Covenant.* New York: Seabury Press.

Bellah, Robert N.
1967 "Civil Religion in America." *Daedalus* 96: 1-21.

Bem, Daryl J.
1970 *Beliefs, Attitudes, and Human Affairs.* Belmont, Ca.: Brooks/Cole.

Benassi, Victor A., Barry Singer and Craig B. Reynolds
1980 "Occult Belief: Seeing is Believing." *Journal for the Scientific Study of Religion* 19: 337-349.

Berger, Peter L.
1984 "Plausibility Structures." Patrick H. McNamara (ed.), Religion: *North American Style.* Belmont, CA: Wadsworth Publishing Company.

Berger, Peter L. and Richard John Neuhaus
1970 *Movement and Revolution.* Garden City, N.Y.: Doubleday and Company, Inc.

Berger, Peter L.
1967 *The Sacred Canopy.* Garden City, N.Y.: Doubleday and Company, Inc.

Berger, Peter L.
1967 "A Sociological View of the Secularization of Theology." *Journal for the Scientific Study of Religion* 6. Spring: 3-16.

Berger, Peter L. and Thomas Luckmann
1967 *The Social Construction of Reality.* New York: Doubleday and Company, Inc.

Berger, Peter L. and Thomas Luckmann
1961 "The Noise of Solemn Assemblies." *Sociology and Social Research* 47.

Berger, Peter L. and Richard John Neuhaus
1970 *Movement and Revolution.* Garden City, N.Y.: Doubleday and Company, Inc.

Bevins, George M.
1983 *The Creationist Movement: Science, Religion and Ideology.* Western Michigan University: Unpublished master's thesis.

Blau, Peter M. and Otis Dudley Duncan
1967 *The American Occupational Structure.* New York: John Wiley & Sons, Inc.

Boettner, Loraine
1977 *"Postmillennialism"* in the Meaning of the Millennium: Four Views, ed. Robert G. Clouse. Downers Grove, IL: Intervarsity Press.

Brehm, Jack W. and Arthur R. Cohen
1962 *Explorations in Cognitive Dissonance.* New York: John Wiley & Sons, Inc.

Budd, Susan
1973 *Sociologists and Religion.* London: Collier-Macmillan.

Cable, Sherry
1984 "Professionalization in Social Movement Organization: A Case Study of Pennsylvanians for Biblical Morality." *Sociological Focus.* Vol 17. No. 4, October.

Carnell, John Edward
1969 *The Case for Biblical Christianity.* Grand Rapids, MI: Eerdmans Publishing Company.

Chafer, Louis Sperry
1947 *Systematic Theology.* 8 vols. Dallas, TX: Dallas Seminary Press.

Chalfant, H. Paul, Robert E. Beckley, and C. Eddie Palmer
1981 *Religion in Contemporary Society.* Sherman Oakes, CA: Alfred Publishing Company.

Clabaugh, Gary K.
   1974 *Thunder on the Right*. Chicago: Nelson-Hall Company.

Cole, Stewart G.
   1971 *The History of Fundamentalism*. Westport, CT: Greenwood Press
        Publishers.

Conway, Flo and Jim Siegelman
   1982 *Holy Terror: The Fundamentalist War on America's Freedom in
        Religion, Politics and Our Private Lives*. Garden City, NY:
        Doubleday and Company, Inc.

Coser, Lewis A. and Bernard Rosenberg
   1957 *Sociological Theory: A Book of Readings*. New York: Macmillan
        Company.

Cox, Harvey
   1984 *Religion in the Secular City: Toward a Postmodern Theology*. New
        York: Simon and Schuster.

Crawford, A.
   1980 *Thunder on the Right*. New York: Pantheon Books.

Darby, John
   1971 *The Collected Writings of Darby*, ed. William Kelly. 34 vols. (reprint,
        Sunbury, PA: Believer's Bookshelf, 1971) 2: 564-573.

Demerath, N. J. and Phillip E. Hammond
   1969 *Religion in Social Context*. New York: Random House.

Demerath, N. J.
   1965 *Social Class in American Protestantism*. Chicago: Rand McNally.

Douglas, Mary
   1966 *Purity and Danger: An Analysis of Concepts of Pollution and Taboo*.
        London: Routledge and Kegan Paul.

Driedger, Leo, Ramond Currie, and Rick Linden
   1983 "Dualistic and Wholistic Views of God and the World: Consequences
        for Social Action." *Review of Religious Research*. 24, 3, March:
        225-244.

Dunford F. and Phillip Kunz
   1973 "The Neutralization of Religious Dissonance." *Review of Religious
        Research* 15:2-9.

Eister, A. W.
1957 "Religious Institutions in Complex Societies: Difficulties in the Theoretic Specification of Functions." *American Sociological Review* 22: 387-389.

Ellsworth, Ralph E. and Sarah M. Harris
1962 *The American Right Wing*. Washington, D.C.: Public Affairs Press.

Falwell, Jerry
1981 "An Interview with the Lone Ranger of American Fundamentalism." *Christianity Today*. September 4, pp 22-29.

Falwell, Jerry
1981 *The Fundamentalist Phenomenon*. Garden City, NY: Doubleday and Company, Inc.

Falwell, Jerry
1981 *The Resurgence of Conservative Christianity*. Garden City, NY: Doubleday and Company, Inc.

Falwell, Jerry
1980 *Listen, America!* New York: Bantam Books.

Feldman, Shel
1966 "Motivational Aspects of Attitudinal Elements and their Place in Cognitive Interaction." Shel Feldman (ed.), *Cognitive Consistency: Motivational Antecedents and Behavioral Consequences*. New York: Academic Press.

Fenn, Richard
1972 "Toward a New Sociology of Religion." *Journal for the Scientific Study of Religion* 11, 1 (March): 16-32.

Festinger, Leon
1957 *Theory of Cognitive Dissonance*. Stanford: Stanford University Press.

Fishbein, Martin
1966 "The Relationships Between Beliefs, Attitudes, and Behavior." Shel Feldman (ed.), *Cognitive Consistency*. New York: Academic Press.

Fowler, Robert Booth
1982 *A New Engagement*. Grand Rapids, MI: William B. Eerdmans Publishing Company.

Gaddy, Gary D.
  1982 "The Power of the Religious Media: Religious Broadcast Use and Role of Religious Organization in Public Affairs." Paper presented to the Society for the Scientific Study of Religion.

Gannon, Thomas M.
  1981 "The New Christian in America as a Social and Political Force." Paper presented to the 1981 meeting for the Association for the Sociology of Religion, Chicago.

Gasper, Louis
  1963 *The Fundamentalist Movement*. Mouton: The Hauge.

Gatewood, Willard B.
  1969 *Controversy in the Twenties*. Nashville, TN: Vanderbilt University Press.

Geisler, Norman L.
  1985 "A Premillennial View of Law and Government," *Bibliodeco Sucra*, July-September. Dallas, TX.

Glock, Charles Y.
  1973 *Religion in Sociological Perspective*. Belmont, CA: Wadsworth Publishing Company, Inc.

Goblot, Edmond
  1965 "Class and Occupation." Pp. 535-540 in Talcott Parsons, Edward Shils, Kaspar D. Naegele, and Jesse R. Pitts (ed.), *Theories of Society*. New York: The Free Press.

Goldthorpe, John H.
  1980 *Social Mobility and Class Structure*. Oxford: Clarendon Press.

Goldthorpe, John H. and Keith Hope
  1974 *The Social Grading of Occupations*. Oxford: Clarendon Press.

Goodman, William R. and James Price
  1981 *Jerry Falwell: An Unauthorized Profile*. Lynchburg, VA: Educational Services.

Goody, J.
  1961 "Religion and Ritual--The Definitional Problem." *British Journal of Sociology* 12: 142-164.

Grabb, Edward G.
  1979 "Working-Class Authoritarianism and Tolerance of Outgroups: A Reassessment." *Public Opinion Quarterly*.

Gusfield, Joseph R.
   1963 *Symbolic Crusade: Status Politics and the American Temperance Movement.* Urbana, IL: University of Illinois Press.

Guth, James L.
   1983 "Southern Baptist Clergy: Vanguard of the Christian Right?" Robert C. Liebman and Robert Wuthnow (ed.), *The New Christian Right.* New York: Aldine Publishing Company.

Hadden, Jeffrey K.
   1985 "Religious Broadcasting and the Mobilization of the New Christian Right." Presidential address delivered to the Society for the Scientific Study of Religion, October 26, 1985, Savannah, GA.

Hadden, Jeffrey K.
   1971 *Religion in Radical Transition.* New York: Aldine Publishing Company.

Hadden, Jeffrey K.
   1970 *The Gathering Storm in the Churches.* Garden City, NY: Doubleday and Company, Inc.

Hadden, Jeffrey K. and Charles F. Longino
   1974 *Gideon's Gang: A Case Study of the Church and Social Action.* Philadelphia: United Church Press.

Hadden, Jeffrey K. and Charles E. Swann
   1981 *Prime Time Preachers.* Reading, MA: Addison Wesley.

Hamilton, Richard F.
   1972 *Class and Politics in the United States.* New York: John Wiley & Sons, Inc.

Hammond, Phillip E.
   1983 "Another Great Awakening?" Robert Wuthnow (ed.), *The New Christian Right.* New York: Aldine Publishing Company.

Hargrove, Barbara
   1979 *The Sociology of Religion.* Arlington Heights, IL: AHM Publishing Corporation.

Harper, Charles L. and Kevin Leicht
   1983 "Religious Belief, Religious Identity and Political Values: The Social Meaning of the New Religious Right." Unpublished manuscript.

Harrell, David Edwin
    1981 "The Roots of the Moral Majority: Fundamentalism Revisited."
        Occasional Papers, Institute for Ecumenical and Cultural Research.

Harrington, Michael
    1983 *The Politics of God's Funeral.* Holt, Rinehart and Winston: New
        York.

Hatch, Nathan O.
    1977 *The Sacred Cause of Liberty.* New Haven, CT: Yale University
        Press.

Hatch, Nathan O. and Mark A. Noll
    1982 *The Bible in America.* New York, NY: Oxford University Press.

Heider, Franz
    1958 *The Psychology of Interpersonal Relations.* New York: John Wiley
        & Sons, Inc.

Henry, Carl F. H.
    1981 "Interview With." *Christianity Today* 2515 (March 13, 1981): 21, 22.

Henry, Carl
    1964 *Aspects of Christian Social Ethics.* Grand Rapids, MI: W. B.
        Eerdmans Publishing Co.

Hill, Samuel S. and Dennis E. Owen
    1982 *The New Religious Political Right in America.* Nashville, TN:
        Abingdon Press.

Himmelstein, Jerome L.
    1983 "The New Right." Robert Wuthnow (ed.), *The New Christian Right.*
        New York: Aldine Publishing Company.

Hofstadter, Richard
    1966 *The Paranoid Style of American Politics.* New York, NY: Alfred A.
        Knopf.

Hofstadter, Richard
    1962 *Anti-Intellectualism in American Life.* New York: Random House.

Hoge, Dean R. and David A. Roozen
    1979 *Understanding Church Growth and Decline, 1950-78.* New York:
        Pilgrim Press.

Johnson, Benton
1972 "On Church and Sect." Joseph E. Faulkner (ed.), *Religion's Influence in Contemporary Society*. Columbus, OH: Charles E. Merrill Publishing Company.

Johnson, Stephen D. and Joseph Tamney
1982 "The Christian Right and the 1982 Presidential Election." *Journal for the Scientific Study of Religion*. Vol. 2: 123-131.

Jorstad, Erling
1984 "Christians and Politics." *Lutheran Standard*, Jan. 6.

Jorstad, Erling
1981 *Evangelicals in the White House: The Cultural Maturation of Born Again Christianity 1960-81*. New York: Edwin Mellen Press.

Jorstad, Erling
1970 *The Politics of Doomsday*. Nashville, TN: Abingdon Press.

Kantzer, Kenneth S. and Stanley N. Gundry
1979 *Perspectives on Evangelical Theology*. Grand Rapids, MI: Baker Book House.

Kater, John L.
1982 *Christians on the Right: the Moral Majority in Perspective*. New York: The Seabury Press.

Kelley, Dean
1984 "Why Conservative Churches are Still Growing." Patrick McNamara (ed.), *Religion: North American Style*. Belmont, CA: Wadsworth Publishing Company.

Kelley, Dean
1972 *Why Conservative Churches are Growing*. San Francisco: Harper and Row.

Knoke, David
1976 *Change and Continuity in American Politics*. Baltimore: Johns Hopkins University Press.

Knoke, David
1973 "Intergenerational Occupational Mobility and the Political Party Preferences of American Men." *American Journal of Sociology* 78:

Knoke, David and James R. Wood
1981 *Organized for Action*. New Brunswick, NY: Rutgers University Press.

Koenig, Thomas and Tracey Boyce
    1983 "Corporate Financing of the Christian Right." Presented at the Society
    for the Scientific Study of Religion, Knoxville, TN, October.

Kohn, Melvin L.
    1977 *Class and Conformity*. Chicago: University of Chicago Press.

Lefever, Harry G.
    1984 "The Religion of the Poor: Escape or Creative Force?" Patrick
    McNamara (ed.), *Religion: North American Style*. Belmont, CA:
    Wadsworth Publishing Company.

Lenski, Gerhard
    1963 *The Religious Factor*. Garden City, NY: Anchor Books, Doubleday
    and Company, Inc.

Liebman, Robert C.
    1983 "Mobilizing the Moral Majority." Robert C. Liebman and Robert
    Wuthnow (eds.), *The New Christian Right*. New York: Aldine.

Liebman, Robert C. and Robert Wuthnow (Eds.)
    1983 *The New Christian Right*. New York: Aldine.

Lipset, Seymour Martin and Earl Raab
    1982 "The Election and the Evangelicals." Pp. 60-71 in H. Uetter, (ed.),
    Speak Out Against the New Right. Boston: Beacon Press.

Lipset, Seymour Martin and Earl Raab
    1981 "The Election and the Evangelicals." *Commentary*. Vol. 71: 25-31.

Lipset, Seymour Martin and Earl Raab
    1970 *The Politics of Unreason*. New York, New York: Harper and Row.

Lipset, Seymour Martin
    1963 *Political Man: The Social Bases of Politics*. Garden City, NY:
    Anchor Books, Doubleday and Company, Inc.

Lofland, John
    1966 *Doomsday Cult*. Englewood Cliffs, NJ: Prentice Hall.

Lorentzen, Louise J.
    1980 "Evangelical Life Style Concerns Expressed in Political Action."
    Patrick H. McNamara (ed.), *Religion: North American Style*.
    Belmont, CA: Wadsworth Publishing Company.

Maguire, Daniel C.
    1982 *The New Subversives*. New York, NY: Continuum Publishing
    Company.

Marsden, George M.
1980 *Fundamentalism and American Culture*. New York, NY: Oxford University Press.

Martin, David
1978 *A General Theory of Secularization*. New York: Harper and Row.

Marty, Martin E.
1960 "Sects and Cults." *The Annals of the American Academy of Political and Social Science* 332: 125-134.

Marty, Martin E.
1980 "Fundamentalism Reborn: Faith and Fanaticism."*Saturday Review*, May:37-42.

Mayer, Helen et al.
1980 "A Tide of Born-Again Politics." *Newsweek*, Sept. 15.

McGuire, Meredith B.
1981 *Religion: The Social Context*. Belmont, CA: Wadsworth Publishing Company.

McGuire, William J.
1960 "Direct and Indirect Persuasive Effects of Dissonance Producing Messages." *Journal of Abnormal and Social Psychology* 60: 354-358.

McIntyre, Thomas J.
1979 *The Fear Brokers*. New York: The Pilgrim Press.

McLoughlin, William G.
1978 *Revivals, Awakenings, and Reform*. Chicago: University of Chicago Press.

McLoughlin, William G. and Robert N. Bellah (Eds.)
1968 *Religion in America*. Boston: Houghton Miflin Company.

McNall, Scott G.
1975 *Career of a Radical Rightist*. Port Washington, NY: Kennikat Press.

Menendez, Albert J.
1977 *Religion at the Polls*. Philadelphia: Westminister Press.

Merton, Robert K.
1967 *Social Theory and Social Structure*. New York: The Free Press.

Minnery, Tom
    1981 "The Man Behind the Mask: Bandit or Crusader?" *Christianity Today*, Sept. 4, 28-29.

Moberg, David
    1972 *The Great Reversal: Evangelism vs. Social Concern.* Philadelphia, PA: Lippincott.

Nash, George H.
    1979 *The Conservative Intellectual Movement in America Since 1945.* New York: Basic Books.

Nelson, Hart M., William E. Snizek and Rodney Stark
    1972 "The Economics of Piety: Religious Commitment and Class." *Sociology and Social Research*, April: 279-289.

Neuhaus, John Richard
    1984 *The Naked Public Square.* 2nd ed. Grand Rapids, MI: William B. Eerdmans Publishing Company.

Neuhaus, John Richard
    1982 "Religion and...Addressing the Naked Public Square." *Worldview*, January.

Newport, Frank
    1979 "The Religious Switcher in the United States." *American Sociological Review*, August: 528-552.

Niebuhr, H. Richard
    1932 "Fundamentalism." P. 527 in *Encyclopaedia of the Social Sciences.*

Niebuhr, H. Richard
    1929 *The Social Sources of Denominationalism.* New York: Holt.

Niebuhr, H. Richard
    1927 *Does Civilization Need Religion: A Study in the Social Resources and Limitations in Religion in Modern Life.* New York: The MacMillan Company.

Noll, Mark A., Nathan O. Hatch, and George M. Marsden
    1984 *The Search for Christian America.* Westchester, IL: Crossway Books.

O'Dea, Thomas F.
    1966 *The Sociology of Religion.* Englewood Cliffs, NJ: Prentice-Hall, Inc.

Ogburn, William F.
1962 *Social Change*. New York: Viking Press.

Osgood, C.E. and P. Tannenbaum
1955 *The Principle of Congruity and the Prediction of Attitude Change.*
Psychological Review. :42-55.

Ostling, Richard N.
1985 "Jerry Falwell's Crusade." *Time*, Sept. 2.

Page, Ann L. and Donald A. Clelland
1978 "Kanawha County Textbook Controversy: A Study of the Politics of
Life Style Concern." *Social Forces* 57: 265-81.

Parsons, Talcott
1974 "Religion in Post-Industrial America: The Problem of Secularization."
Social Research 41: 193-225.

Patel, Kant and Denny Pilant
1982 "The Politics of the New Christian Right: Study of Born-Again
Christians in a Border State." Paper delivered to the Society for the
Scientific Study of Religion, Providence, RI.

Perry, Everett L.
1959 "The Role of Socio-Economic Factors in the Rise and Development of
American Fundamentalism." Unpublished doctoral dissertation,
University of Chicago.

Petersen, William J. and Stephen Board
1980 "Where is Jerry Falwell Going?" Pp. 18-19 in *Eternity*.

Pierard, Richard V.
1983 "Religion and the New Right in Contemporary American Politics."
Religion and Politics, ed. James Wood, Jr. Institute of Church-State
Studies.

Pierard, Richard V.
1983 "No Hoosier Hospitality for Humanism: The Moral Majority in
Indiana." Paper presented at the Society for the Scientific Study of
Religion, Providence, RI.

Pierard, Richard V.
1970 *The Unequal Yoke*. Philadelphia: B. Lippincott Company.

Plowman, Edward E.
1979 "Is Morality All Right?" *Christianity Today*, 23 (November 2) :76-
85.

Pope, Liston
1942 *Millhands and Preachers*. New Haven: Yale University Press.

Prus, Robert C.
1976 "Religous Recruitment and the Management of Dissonance: A Sociological Perspective." *Sociological Inquiry* 46: 127-134.

Quebedeaux, Richard
1982 *By What Authority?* San Francisco: Harper and Row.

Quebedeaux, Richard
1978 *The Worldly Evangelicals*. San Francisco: Harper and Row.

Quebedeaux, Richard
1974 *The Young Evangelicals*. New York: Harper and Row.

Quinley, Harold E.
1974 *The Prophetic Clergy: Social Action Among Protestant Ministers*. New York.

Roberts, Keith A.
1984 *Religion in Sociological Perspective*. Homewood, IL: The Dorsey Press.

Rossiter, Clinton
1966 *The Grand Convention*. New York: MacMillan.

Russell, C. Allyn
1976 *Voices of American Fundamentalism*. Philadelphia: The Westminster Press.

Sandeen, Ernest
1970 *The Roots of Fundamentalism*. Chicago: University of Chicago Press.

Sandeen, Ernest R.
1970 "Fundamentalism and American Identity." Annals of the American Academy of Political and Social Science. January, :56-65.

Sandeen, Ernest
1968 *Origins of Fundamentalism*. Philadelphia: Fortress Press.

Scharf, Betty R.
1970 *The Sociological Study of Religion*. London: Hutchinson University Library.

Schoenberger, Robert A.
    1969 *The American Right Wing.* New York, NY: Holt, Rinehart and Winston, Inc.

Shiner, Larry
    1967 "The Concept of Secularization in Empirical Research." *Journal for the Scientific Study of Religion*;207-220.

Shriver, Peggy L., Anson Shupe and William Stacey
    1982 "Correlates of Support for the Electronic Church." *Journal for the Scientific Study of Religion* 21: 291-303.

Shriver, Peggy L.
    1981 *The Bible Vote: Religion and the New Right.* New York: Pilgrim Press.

Shupe, Anson and Susan Stacey
    1982 *Born Again Politics and the Moral Majority: What Social Surveys Really Show.*Lewiston, New York: Edwin Mellen Press.

Shupe, Anson and Susan Stacey
    1981 "Religious Values and Religiosity in the Textbook Adoption Controversy in Texas." Paper presented at the annual meeting of the Society for the Scientific Study of Religion, October, 1982. Providence, RI.

Simpson, John H.
    1983 "Moral Issues and Status Politics." Robert C. Liebman and Robert Wuthnow (eds.), *The New Christian Right.* New York: Aldine.

Smith, W. Robertson
    1965 "Jehovah and the Prophets." Pp. 661-664 in Talcott Parsons, Edward Shils, Kaspar D. Naegele, and Jesse R. Pitts (eds.), *Theories of Society.* New York: The Free Press.

Snow, David A. and Richard Machalek
    1982 "On The Presumed Fragility of Unconventional Beliefs." *Journal for the Scientific Study of Religion*, 21(1): 15-26.

Sorokin, Pitirim A.
    1965 "Social Stratification." Pp. 570-576 in Talcott Parsons, Edward Shils, Kaspar D. Naegele, and Jesse R. Pitts (eds.), *Theories of Society.* New York: The Free Press.

Stacks, John F.
    1981 "It's Rightward On." *Time*, June 1.

Stark, Rodney and Charles Glock
     1968 *American Piety*. Berkeley, CA: University of California Press.

Stark, Rodney, Bruce D. Foster, Charles Y. Glock and Harold Quinley
     1971 *Wayward Shepherds*. New York: Harper and Row.

Szasz, Ferenc Morton
     1982 *The Divided Mind of Protestant America, 1880-1930*. University,
          Alabama: The University of Alabama Press.

Tamney, Joseph B. and Stephen D. Johnson
     1982 "The Moral Majority in Middletown." Paper presented at the Society
          for the Scientific Study of Religion, Providence, RI.

Troeltsch, Ernst
     1931 *The Social Teaching of the Christian Churches*. New York: Macmillan
          Company.

Verba, Sidney and Norman H. Nie
     1972 *Participation in America: Political Democracy and Social Equality*.
          New York: Harper and Row.

Viguerie, Richard A.
     1981 *The New Right: We're Ready to Lead*. Falls Church, VA: The
          Viguerie Company.

Warner, William Lloyd
     1949 *Democracy in Jonesville*. New York: Harper and Row.

Webber, Robert E.
     1981 *The Moral Majority: Right or Wrong?* Westchester, IL: Cornerstone
          Books.

Weber, Max
     1963 *The Sociology of Religion*. Boston: Beacon Press. Translated by
          Ephraim Fischoff.

Weber, Max
     1958 *The Protestant Ethic and the Spirit of Capitalism*. New York: Charles
          Scribner's Sons.

Weber, Max
     1946 C. Wright Mills (ed.), From Max Weber, *Essays in Sociology*. New
          York: Oxford University Press.

Weber, Timothy
    1982 "The Two-Edged Sword: The Fundamentalist Use of the Bible" in Nathan O. Hatch and Mark A. Noll, *The Bible in America*. New York: Oxford University Press.

Wells, David F. and John D. Woodbridge (Eds.)
    1975 *The Evangelicals*. Nashville, TN: Abingdon Press.

Wilson, Bryan
    1966 *Religion in Secular Society*. London: Watts.

Wood, James R.
    1984 "Leaders, Values, and Societal Change." *Sociological Analysis* 45: 1-9.

Wood, James R.
    1981 *Leadership in Voluntary Organizations: The Controversy over Social Action in Protestant Churches*. New Brunswick, NJ: Rutgers University Press.

Wuthnow, Robert
    1981 "Two Traditions in the Study of Religion." *Journal for the Scientific Study of Religion* 20: 16-32.

Wuthnow, Robert
    1973 "Religious Commitment and Conservatism: In Search of an Elusive Relationship." Pp. 117-132 in Charles Glock (ed.) *Religion in Sociological Perspective*. Belmont, CA: Wadsworth Publishing Company.

Wuthnow, Robert
    1973 "The Political Rebirth of American Evangelicals." Robert C. Liebman and Robert Wuthnow (eds.), *The New Christian Right*. New York: Aldine Publishing Company.

Yankelovich, Daniel
    1981 "New Rules in American Life: Searching for Self-Fulfillment in a World Turned Upside Down." *Psychology Today* (April): 35-91.

Yinger, J. Milton and Stephen J. Cutler
    1982 "The Moral Majority Viewed Sociologically." *Sociological Focus* 15: 289-306.

Young, Perry D.
    1982 *God's Bullies: Native Reflections on Preachers and Priorities*. New York: Holt, Rinehart and Winston.

Zurcher, Louis A. Jr., R. G. Kirkpatrick, R. G. Cushing and C. K. Bowman
      1971 "The Anti-Pornography Campaign: A Symbolic Crusade." *Social Problems* 19: 217-38.

Zwier, Robert and Richard Smith
      1980 "Christian Politics and the New Right." *Christian Century* (October 8) Vol. 97, Mo. 31: 937-941.

Index

STUDIES IN RELIGION AND SOCIETY